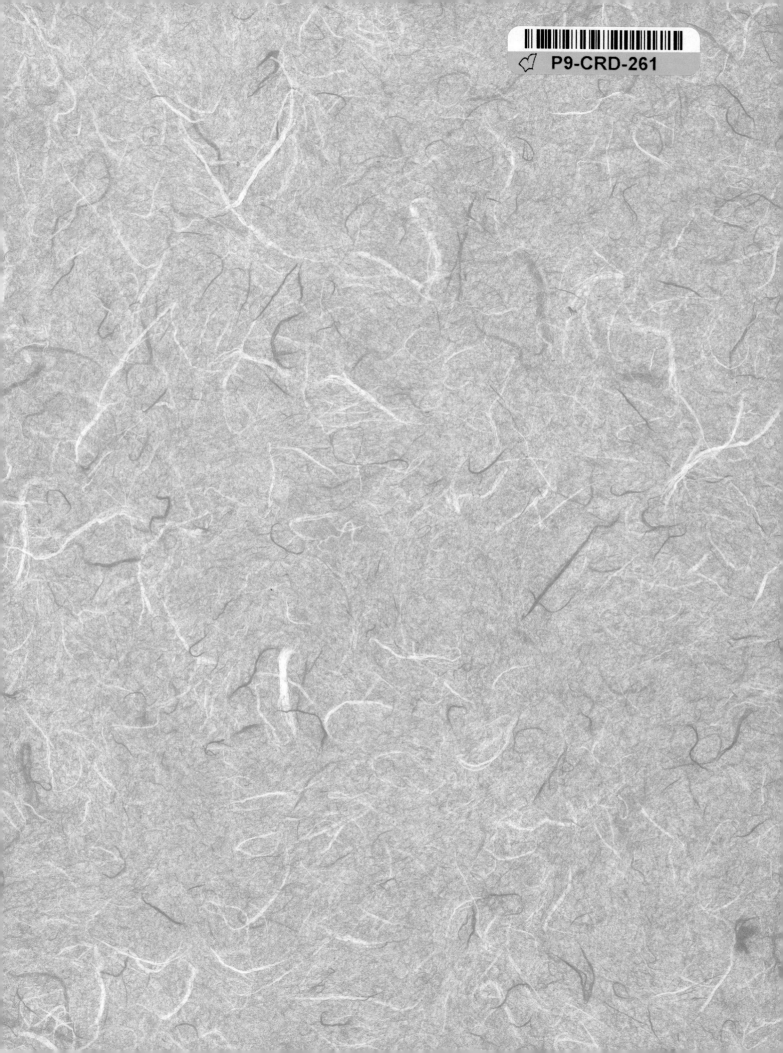
P9-CRD-261

SIMPLY CHINESE

MORE THAN 60
QUICK AND EASY RECIPES
FROM CHINA

SIMPLY CHINESE

More Than 60
Quick and Easy Recipes
From China

MARGARET Y. LEUNG

ACKNOWLEDGMENTS

Valuable assistance was provided by the following individuals and organizations: Judi Adams and Margie Martin at the Wheat Foods Council; Alison Athens at the Peanut Advisory Board; Kay Engelhardt at the American Egg Board; Margie Frate and Anita Keeler at Caryl Saunders Associates for the Chilean Winter Fruit Association and the Fresh Garlic Association; Emily Holt and Clare Vanderbeek at the National Fisheries Institute; Mary Jo Hogue at the Rice Council; Anita Hudson at Michigan Asparagus Advisory Board; Robin Kline and Anne Rehnstrom at National Pork Producers Council; Karen Lobb of Oregon Hazelnuts; Molly Machamer at United Fresh Fruit and Vegetable Association; Susan Mesick of Ketchum Public Relations for the Mushroom Council; Natalie Quizon and Eric Skiba; Gail Rolka, for typing the manuscript; Priscilla Root at the American Lamb Council; Janet Stern at the National Live Stock and Meat Board; Dot Tringali at Newman Saylor & Gregory for the National Broiler Council; Peter Wildhorn and Hui Fen.

Copyright © 1993 Bluewood Books

Published by Longmeadow Press, 201 High Ridge Road, Stamford, CT 06904. All rights reserved. No part of this book may be reproduced or utilized in any form or by any means, electronic or mechanical, including photocopying, recording or by any information storage and retrieval system, without permission in writing from the Publisher.

Cover and interior design by
  Tom Debolski
Edited by Lynne Piade
Food Consultant: Meesha Halm
Contributing Writer: Bill Yenne

ISBN: 0-681-41735-8

Printed in Hong Kong

First Longmeadow Press Edition 1993

0 9 8 7 6 5 4 3 2 1

Page 2: Scenic rice fields of China's heartland.

Page 3: Traditional Lamb Stir-fry (recipe on page 35).

CONTENTS

FOUR SEASONAL MENUS

SPRING
HOT AND SOUR SOUP WITH BEEF *page 18*
CHICKEN SALAD WITH GRAPES *page 22*
SEAFOOD AND ASPARAGUS STIR-FRY *page 45*
GINGER PORK WITH PEANUT SAUCE *page 37*
RICE *page 58*

SUMMER
BAKED WONTONS WITH FRESH GINGER SAUCE *page 17*
SESAME PORK APPETIZERS *page 16*
STIR-FRIED MIXED VEGETABLES *page 51*
COLD NOODLES WITH CHICKEN,
HAM, AND CUCUMBER *page 74*

FALL
TWICE-COOKED MEATBALLS WITH PEANUTS,
GINGER, AND SPICY CABBAGE *page 14*
PORK AND VEGETABLE SOUP *page 21*
SHANGHAI BEEF SALAD *page 25*
STEAMED FISH *page 45*
SUBGUM FRIED RICE *page 59*

WINTER
POT STICKERS *page 13*
WON TON SOUP *page 21*
BAKED SPARERIBS *page 37*
HUNAN CHICKEN WITH GARLIC *page 40*
STEAMED RICE *page 58*

INTRODUCTION

Chinese cooks have been developing a low-calorie, well-balanced cuisine over the past four thousand years. Non-starchy vegetables predominate. Lean meat is used sparingly as a flavoring agent rather than as the main ingredient. High-protein seafood and the versatile soy bean play an important nutritional role in the Chinese diet. Grains and vegetables are used in abundance. There are no dairy products like butter or milk, and animal fats are used sparingly. Cooking or stir-frying is done quickly, in very hot peanut or sesame oil or is cooked in its own juices with very little added oil. Stir-frying retains the food's texture, taste, and color. Vegetables remain bright. The hot oil seals in the vegetable's juices, while at the same time extracting its flavor. By cooking in its own juices, the vegetable's valuable vitamin and mineral content is not lost.

For these reasons Chinese cuisine has found a following among those who want to eat healthier, lighter meals and still get their full supply of nutrients without giving up flavor. The deliciously fresh and colorful quality of the food and the convivial style of sharing many dishes among friends and family make Chinese cooking a joy for anyone. Each of the savory recipes in *SIMPLY CHINESE* will excite your palate with new tastes and exotic flavors using some familiar and some new ingredients.

China is called by its people, the Middle Flowery People's Republic. It is made up of 18 provinces and divided by some of the highest mountain ranges in the world. The

Left: Market day near the Burmese border in Xishuangbanna.

Right: Vegetable Pork Stir-fry (recipe on page 39).

four schools of Chinese cuisine evolved out of what were distinctly regional cooking styles that depended on locally available ingredients: northern, eastern, southwestern, and southern.

In the north, wheat, not rice, is the main agricultural product. In the northern school, wheat flour, from which is made many noodle dishes, steamed bread, and dumplings, naturally permeates this cuisine. Beijing (Peking) was the capital of China for many centuries, and its cuisine reflected the fact that the emperor and his courtiers recruited the best chefs in China and encouraged them to develop new and imaginative dishes. Northern food tends generally to be lighter and includes both sweet-and-sour dishes and more subtle, delicately seasoned food. Beijing and its neighboring districts use wine stock in their dishes, and season with garlic and green onions. Probably the most famous of the northern delicacies is the celebrated Peking duck. Today, China's northern culinary region includes all of Hebei (Hopei) province, Shandong (Shantung) province, and Honan (Henan) province.

Much of the north is bordered by Mongolia. When the Mongols invaded China in the thirteenth century and set up a dynasty which ruled from 1279 to 1368, they brought lamb and their hot pot cooking techniques with them. Both have remained favorites in that region ever since. The traditional hot pot is a round metal bowl containing water or stock. In the center is a chimney. Underneath is a built-in brazier filled with charcoal. As the charcoal ignites, the stock boils and each diner dips uncooked sliced meats and vegetables into the boiling liquid. (This cooks the food and flavors the stock which is consumed last.) The food is then dipped into sauces which flavor and cool it before eating. Mutton or lamb is the basis of the Mongolian hot pot, but in other provinces where lamb is not popular, chicken, beef, pork, shrimp, spinach, bok choy, and clams might be substituted. There is also the Mon-

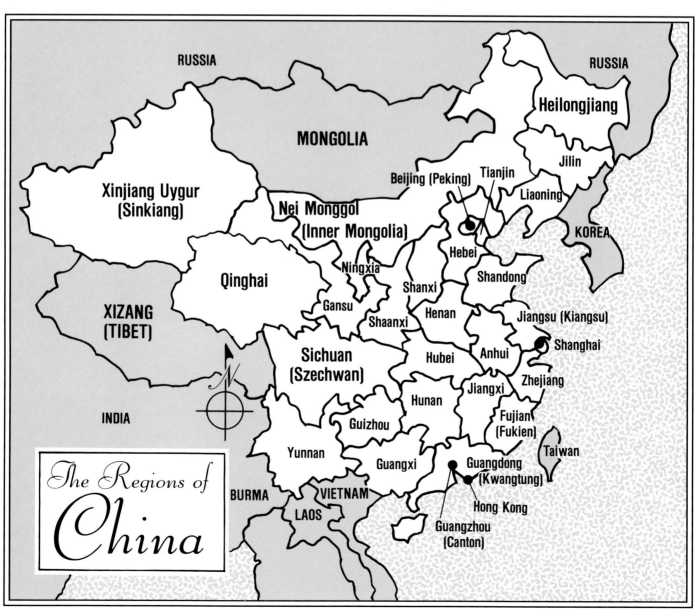

The Regions of China

golian grill, an indoor barbecue upon which long, thin strips of spiced meat are roasted on a red-hot grill over an open charcoal fire. The strips are then served over a bed of fried rice noodles or with plain buns. Both styles of do-it-yourself cooking are good for feasts.

In the coastal area around Shanghai and further south, rice flour replaces wheat flour as the staple. The cooks on the east coast use more soy sauce and sugar, and specialize in salty and gravy-laden dishes. Fish and shellfish from the many rivers and neighboring seas are, naturally, popular ingredients, as are lots of vegetables.

Fujian (Fukien) province, on the eastern seaboard, has long been considered its own gastronomical region and is famous for its seafood and clear, light soups. Fujian also produces the best soy sauce, and stewing in this sauce, or "red cooking" as it is called, very popular. Fujian is also famous for its pork and chicken dishes made with sweet-tasting red fermented rice paste, and for its soft spring rolls. Today, Zhejiang (Chekiang) province and its capitol, Shanghai, and Jiangsu (Kiangsu) province are all considered part of China's eastern culinary region.

The inland regions of Sichuan (Szechwan), Yunnan, and Hunan are noted for a locally grown, piquant pepper called fagara. It is used most often with red cooked meat and poultry. Chilies, too, are typical flavor enhancers in Sichuan cuisine. They are red or green and very strong and hot. The spicy flavoring of Sichuan dishes is unmistakable. The most characteristic dishes of the region are chicken with peanuts and hot pepper, diced pork with fish flavor, and carp with hot bean sauce.

Guangzhou (Canton), a southern seaport, has always been a city of commerce and travel. It was also the destination of the emperor's chefs who fled south at the overthrow of the Ming Dynasty in 1644. For this reason and partly because of its abundant natural resources, Guangzhou has perhaps the most varied cuisine in China. Today, China's southern culinary region includes Guangdong (Kwangtung) province and the area around Guangzhou. In the south, they delicately prepare many varieties of fresh vegetables and seafood. Pork and poultry is prefered roasted or grilled and seasoned with nuts and mushrooms. Steamed dishes, too, are popular. The southerners are famous for dim sum, steamed dumplings stuffed with meat or seafood, sweet paste, or preserves that are eaten as an early morning or lunchtime snack. The Chinese delicacies Westerners know best, such as eggrolls, egg foo young, and roast pork, are from Guangzhou.

With a little practice using this cookbook, you will be able to prepare Chinese recipes with traditional flavor in no time at all. The number of servings each recipe will yeild is based on the Western idea of serving one main dish. However, family-style Chinese meals are composed of a number of dishes that are brought to the table at once. They usually include a rice or noodle dish. While at first you may not be able to coordinate the cooking of a feast, you may want to serve your dish with hot, steamed white rice.

THE INFLUENCE OF GUANGZHOU IN AMERICA

The first major migration of Chinese to America came in the second half of the 1800s when gold was discovered in California and railroads were the all-consuming passion and industry of the time. Most were southern farm boys from the rural districts around Guangzhou who were recruited to work on the transcontinental railroads. By mid-1866 more than 6000 Chinese were working on the Central Pacific. Today San Francisco's Chinatown remains the largest gathering of Chinese outside of mainland China, and in America, the dominant Chinese culture is Guangzhounese.

While the official language of China is Mandarin, subdialects are spoken all over the country. Written Mandarin remains unaffected by dialect; each character stands for one word. But transliterating Mandarin into English poses a problem—whose dialect do we choose? With the overwhelming Guangzhounese influence in America and outside of China, scholars have settled on the Wade-Giles translation system, which favors Guangzhounese pronunciation. For example, Peking is pronounced as it is spelled. However, Pinyin translation, which is closer to mainland pronunciation, would have us pronounce Peking as Beijing.

While examining the language is one way to learn about a country's cultural differences, sampling regional dishes is another, and one that can be extremely satisfying.

THE BASICS

Sharing food is so important to Chinese culture that a common greeting is "Have you eaten rice yet?"

A Chinese meal is rather like a buffet, at which a guest eats little bits of this and that, rather than a large portion of just one food. Chinese dishes are not served in individual

Peppers for sale at a Xishuangbanna market

portions, but are on platters shared by all those who sit at the table. Everyone can—indeed is expected to—eat from all the dishes presented.

A proper dinner includes at least one fowl, one fish, and one meat dish, which are in turn complemented with appropriate vegetables. All the dishes are brought to the table at once and eaten together. A well-prepared Chinese dish is expected to contain five basic flavors: salty, sour, sweet, hot, and fragrant. It should appeal to more senses than the one of taste. Its colors should be pleasing to the eye, the ingredients should be of uniform size, and it should be fragrant. Chefs have been known to cut fanciful creatures out of mushrooms and stars out of carrots to lend flair and whimsy to a dish. Within the meal there should be contrasting tastes and textures; if one dish is crisp, it should be offset by another that is smooth; a bland dish is paired with a spiced one. Always the effort is to create a balance and harmony.

For vegetables, meats, and fish, a good rule of thumb is that one pound will serve four. Most of the recipes are intended to be served with rice or noodles. If the quantities in a recipe seem small, you may double them if you remember these limitations on stir-frying. When you double a stir-fry recipe, double the main ingredients (meat, fish, vegetables) and increase the liquids and seasonings by a third. You can add more seasoning later if you wish. Increase the cooking time by fifty percent, testing for doneness as you go. If doubling the recipe will be too much for your pan to hold, you must make it simultaneously in two batches using separate woks or skillets, or transfer half to a warm pan or chafing dish while the second half is prepared.

When stir-frying for a large group the key is to cook each ingredient separately so each gets the benefit of the hottest spot in the wok for its cooking period. When the ingredient is crispy-tender, transfer it to a large heated pan to keep it warm while you cook the other ingredients. When all the ingredients have been stir-fried, combine them in the wok for a final heating and serve as soon as possible.

UTENSILS

Chinese cuisine is one of the most economical cuisines in the world. In it there is an economy of movement, space, fuel, and waste. Having the proper utensils makes cooking Chinese food much easier. These basic items will guide you on the path to creating authentic Chinese family feasts.

Wok: A wok is an all-purpose cooking pot with flared sides, a rounded bottom, handles, and a lid. It is made of thin metal that conducts heat quickly and evenly: iron, copper, brass, aluminum, or stainless steel. The rounded-bottom wok fits into a ring or collar that keeps the wok level and works best over a high flame on a gas range. There are also flat bottom woks on the market that rest directly on the heat source and are a good choice for electric ranges. Electric woks are also available but a common complaint is that they respond slowly to changes in temperature. A fairly deep, heavy skillet may be substituted for a wok when stir-frying. But their versatility makes woks a good choice for pan-frying, parboiling, simmering, braising, deep-frying, steaming, and stir-frying.

Cleaver: A sharp knife or cleaver made of tempered steel will serve many purposes in the kitchen. The cleaver has a rectangular blade that is about 3×8 inches. A lighter version is used for slicing softer meats and vegetables while the heavier version is more versatile and will chop through bones, joints, and shellfish casings. With both sizes the blunt thick part of the blade is good for crushing garlic cloves and ginger, and for pounding and tenderizing meat.

Chopping block: The best kind of chopping block is a thick, solid one that won't slide around. Chinese chefs prefer to use one that has been made from a cross section of a tree trunk.

Cooking chopsticks: Bamboo and wooden chopsticks are handy kitchen utensils and with practice can become like extensions of the fingers. They don't conduct heat. Chopsticks don't bruise softer ingredients. They may be used in place of spoons, forks, whisks, and beaters and can lift deep-fried foods out of hot oil.

Rice paddles: For lifting rice out of a steamer without injuring the grains.

Ladles: These are used in the same way you would use any ladle.

Spatula: These are specially curved to use with the wok, but they are used as you would any spatula.

Steamer: Holds vegetables, meats, fish, dim sum, or rice about 2 inches above boiling water inside a deep pot or wok with a tight-fitting lid and allows for moist-heat cooking.

Strainer/skimmer: Good for skimming the fat off the top of a soup or stock, or for lifting fried foods out of deep fat.

Wok brush: A bamboo brush used to clean the wok.

CUTTING TECHNIQUES

In Chinese cooking, great attention is paid to precision cutting and preparation of the ingredients prior to cooking. The reason for this is to reduce the total cooking time. With the ingredients cut the same size or shape they will cook in approximately the same amount of time, and the result will be a hot, delicious dish, with each ingredient properly cooked, none overdone or underdone. It is up to the cook to know the length of cooking time each ingredient requires to bring out its best color, flavor, and texture.

Mincing: Slice the meat across the grain, then cut the slices lengthwise into shreds, and finally, chop across the shreds. Meat that is to be used in meatballs or dumplings should be very finely minced. Minced garlic is often called for in Chinese recipes.

Slicing: Meat should be sliced across the grain into slices about ⅛-inch thick. Chicken breasts still on the bone are sliced horizontally. Cut down along the breast bone as deep as the finished slice is supposed to be thick. Remove the knife and make a cut perpendicular to the first cut.

Cubing: The size of the cubes depends on the dish. Cubing generally refers to food cut in pieces ½-inch thick or larger. This is done by slicing first lengthwise then crosswise. Dicing refers to cubes in pieces ⅛- to ¼-inch on each side.

Matchstick: Matchsticks are thin pieces of meat or vegetables, usually cut against the grain, into pieces about 1½ inches by ⅛ by ⅛-inch.

Scoring: Scoring adds to the visual appeal of the dish and also tenderizes the meat. The size of the pattern and the depth of the cuts vary with each dish, but it should be done at an angle to the grain.

Roll-cutting: is another way to cut stalk vegetables such as carrots and celery. Roll-cutting allows the vegetable to cook quickly and absorb more flavor. Generally, vegetables are cut into pieces the size of the other main ingredients of a dish. Make a diagonal cut straight down. Roll the carrot one-quarter turn and slice again. Continue slicing until all the carrot is cut into triangular-shaped wedges.

APPETIZERS AND DIM SUM

點心

Dim sum means, literally, "delight your heart" and it is served in the morning at Chinese teahouses. Dim sum are dainty delicacies in the form of crescents or buns filled with meat or seafood, steamed in bamboo baskets, and served three to four per basket. Sweet or salty fried pastries also stuffed with bean paste and other treats are served one to four on a plate. Traditionally, dim sum is served by uniformed waitresses known as dim sum maids who push carts, carrying a variety of these appetizers among the diners. They circle constantly, calling out the names of the items on their carts and return often to the kitchen to pick up fresh dim sum. To order, one has merely to point to the item that looks appealing for it to be placed on the table. The bill is figured by the waitress either by counting the number of empty plates, or by marking down each item as it is placed on the table.

STEAMED PORK BUNS

MAKES 20 PAU

Steamed pork buns or *Pau* are typical dim sum offerings.

DOUGH

- 1 package active dry yeast
- ¾ cup water 105° F to 115° F
- 3 cups all-purpose flour
- 3 tablespoons sugar
- 1½ teaspoons baking powder
- 1½ tablespoons shortening

FILLING

- ½ pound ground pork
- 1 pound Chinese cabbage, finely chopped
- ¼ cup chicken broth
- 1 teaspoon salt
- 1 tablespoon sesame oil
- 1 tablespoon soy sauce
- 2 tablespoons grated fresh ginger
- ¾ cup diced onion

Dissolve yeast in water. Add yeast mixture to 2¼ cups flour; mix well. Cover with plastic wrap and let rest for an hour in a warm place.

For filling, combine the ground pork, cabbage, broth, salt, sesame oil, soy sauce, ginger, and onion. Set aside.

Add sugar to dough; with hands work sugar into the dough until sugar is dissolved. Add ¾ cup flour, baking powder, and shortening and continue kneading the dough until smooth. Divide the dough into 20 pieces. Roll each piece into a 4-inch circle. Place about 1 tablespoon filling in the center of each circle; dampen the edges with water. Bring the edges up around the filling, gather the edges into a pouch; pinch together and twist to seal. Place on a 2-inch square of waxed paper. Repeat with remaining circles. Cover and let rise in a warm place for 20 minutes.

Place pau ½-inch apart on a rack in a steamer; cover and steam over boiling water for 12 to 15 minutes. Immediately remove the waxed paper. Serve hot.

Preparation time: 1½ hours
Cooking time: 15 minutes

EGGROLLS

MAKES 6 SERVINGS

·This Cantonese specialty measures 5 to 6 inches and its batter is made with eggs. Eggrolls are served as appetizers or with dinner.

2 to 3   tablespoons vegetable oil
½   pound ground pork
¼   pound shrimp, shelled, deveined, and finely chopped
1   teaspoon minced fresh ginger
½   pound bean sprouts, blanched
½   cup minced green onions
1   tablespoon soy sauce
½   teaspoon salt
12   eggroll skins
1   egg, beaten

In a wok or Dutch oven heat oil. Stir-fry pork until it loses its pink color. Add shrimp, stir-fry for 1 minute. Add bean sprouts and green onions. Add soy sauce and salt; mix well. Transfer mixture to a colander; drain and let cool about 30 minutes.

Place the eggroll skin with one corner facing you. Place 2 tablespoons of filling slightly below the center of the skin. Fold the bottom corner over filling. Fold the left and right corners over the filling. Roll the skin away from you, wrapping securely. Seal the eggroll by brushing the inside top edge with beaten egg. Stack eggrolls on a damp towel and cover with another damp towel until ready to deep-fry.

In a wok or Dutch oven heat oil for deep-frying to 375° F. Add a few eggrolls, reduce heat slightly and deep-fry until golden brown on both sides. Lift out of oil and drain on paper towels, without stacking.

Cut eggrolls in 1½-inch sections or in thirds. Serve with hot mustard, plum sauce, or soy sauce.

Preparation time: 15 minutes
Chilling time: 30 minutes
Cooking time: 20 minutes

POT STICKERS

MAKES 40 POT STICKERS

Pot Stickers are delicious crescent-shaped appetizers filled with ground pork, shrimp, fresh ginger, and other good things.

DOUGH

3   cups all-purpose flour
1   cup water

FILLING

10   ounces ground pork
1   teaspoon salt
1   tablespoon sesame oil
1   tablespoon soy sauce
1   tablespoon grated fresh ginger
1   tablespoon finely chopped green onion
¼   cup chicken broth
½   cup diced shrimp
½   cup finely chopped Chinese cabbage
½   diced mushrooms
2   tablespoons vegetable oil

Blend the flour with 1 cup of water. Cover with plastic wrap and let rest for 30 minutes. Knead the dough for 5 minutes, or until smooth; cover.

Mix the ground pork with salt, sesame oil, soy sauce, ginger, green onion, and broth. Add the shrimp, cabbage, and mushrooms. Mix well.

On a lightly floured surface, roll out the dough to slightly less than a ⅛-inch thickness. Using a cookie cutter, cut the dough into 3-inch rounds, making 35 to 40. (Re-roll dough as needed.) Spoon about 1 heaping teaspoon of filling into the center of each round. For each dumpling, moisten the edge of the round with water; fold round in half. Fold small pleats only along one edge, pressing the pleats against the other edge to seal. Place, pleated side up, on a floured baking sheet; cover.

In a wok or 12-inch skillet with a nonstick coating, heat 1 tablespoon of oil over medium-high heat. Add as many pot stickers as will fit in a single layer without touching. Cook, uncovered, until the bottoms of the pot stickers are crisp and brown, about 5 minutes. Add ¼ cup of water; cover the pan immediately and steam the pot stickers until cooked through, about 8 minutes. Transfer to a warm plate. Repeat with the remaining pot stickers and oil. Serve immediately.

Preparation time: 30 minutes
Cooking time: 15 to 25 minutes

TWICE-COOKED MEATBALLS WITH PEANUTS, GINGER, AND SPICY CABBAGE

MAKES 24 MEATBALLS

MEATBALLS

½　cup roasted and salted peanuts
½　cup diced yellow onion
1　clove garlic, peeled
1　teaspoon minced fresh ginger
½　cup canned water chestnuts
1　pound ground beef
2　teaspoons peanut oil
¼　cup teriyaki sauce
2　tablespoons orange marmalade
1½　bok choy or white cabbage heads, about 1½ quarts, core removed and thinly sliced

PEANUT SAUCE

1　tablespoon sesame oil
1　tablespoon sugar
　　Salt to taste
½　cup roasted and salted peanuts
1　tablespoon minced garlic
1　tablespoon minced fresh ginger
1　cup sliced green onion
2　tablespoons butter
2　tablespoons peanut oil
　　Tabasco sauce to taste
1　cup diced fresh pineapple, to garnish

Preheat the oven to 400° F. Prepare the meatballs: In the bowl of a food processor, combine the peanuts, onion, garlic, ginger, and water chestnuts and process until finely chopped. Combine the peanut mixture with the ground beef and form into meatballs using a 1-ounce scoop (2 tablespoons). Toss the meatballs with the peanut oil and spread them on a baking sheet. Bake the meatballs for about 5 minutes until browned.

Combine the teriyaki sauce and orange marmalade. Drain the meatballs on paper towels. Toss meatballs with teriyaki marmalade sauce. Set aside.

In a wok or medium skillet with a lid, add 2 cups of water and the cabbage. Cook with the lid askew over medium heat until the cabbage is just soft and the water is evaporated. While the cabbage is cooking, prepare the peanut sauce: Combine the ingredients in a small saucepan and sauté over high heat. Stir to lightly toast the peanuts and lightly cook the green onion.

Return the meatballs to the oven to reheat. Toss the hot peanut sauce with the hot cabbage and divide among plates. Top with meatballs. Garnish with the fresh diced pineapple.

Preparation time: 30 minutes
Cooking time: 15 minutes

Twice-cooked Meatballs with Peanuts, Ginger, and Spicy Cabbage

SINGAPORE SAMPLINGS

MAKES 6 SERVINGS

1½   pounds boneless pork loin, sliced
     into 4 × 1 × ⅛-inch strips
¼   cup soy sauce
3   tablespoons rice vinegar
1   tablespoon grated fresh ginger,
     or 1 teaspoon dry ginger
1   clove garlic, minced
½   teaspoon crushed red pepper
     Peppered Tofu (recipe follows),
     if desired
6   wooden skewers

Soak skewers for 10 to 20 minutes in water. Thread pork onto skewers; place in a 12 × 9-inch baking dish. Combine the soy sauce, vinegar, ginger, garlic, and crushed red pepper. Set aside ⅛ cup marinade to baste skewers. Pour remaining marinade over skewers, turning to coat. Marinate at room temperature for 30 minutes, turning one or twice. Broil 6 inches from heat for 10 minutes, turning to cook all sides. Baste occasionally with reserved marinade. Serve with peppered tofu, if desired.

Preparation time: 10 minutes
Marinating time: 30 minutes
Cooking time: 10 minutes

PEPPERED TOFU

1   tablespoon sesame oil
½   teaspoon dried red pepper
1   teaspoon minced fresh ginger
1   tablespoon oyster sauce
8   ounces tofu, cubed

Heat sesame oil in a wok or skillet. Add dried red pepper and fresh ginger. Cook over medium heat for 2 to 3 minutes, stirring constantly. Stir in oyster sauce. Add cubed tofu; stir to heat through and coat with sauce.

Preparation time: 15 minutes
Cooking time: 25 minutes

Singapore Samplings with Peppered Tofu

SESAME PORK APPETIZERS

MAKES 6 SERVINGS

1½ pounds pork tenderloin
½ cup dry sherry
1 tablespoon soy sauce
½ cup honey
½ cup sesame seeds

In a dish large enough to hold the tenderloin, combine the sherry and soy sauce; add the pork. Marinate for 1 to 2 hours, turning several times. Remove the tenderloin. Spread the honey on a plate. Roll the pork in the honey, then in the sesame seeds. Place the tenderloin in a roasting pan; roast at 350° F for 20 minutes, or until the meat thermometer registers 155° F. Let stand 5 minutes, then slice thinly on the diagonal.

Preparation time: 15 minutes
Marinating time: 1 to 2 hours
Cooking time: 25 minutes

DIPPING SAUCE

⅓ cup soy sauce
1 tablespoon dry sherry
1 clove garlic, crushed
½ teaspoon grated fresh ginger
1 green onion, finely chopped
Spinach leaves, to garnish

In a small bowl, combine all the ingredients for dipping sauce. Place the bowl in the center of a serving platter. Surround the bowl with the spinach leaves. Arrange pork slices on top.

PORK KABOBS *Very good*

MAKES 6 SERVINGS

½ cup unsweetened
　　pineapple juice
¼ cup soy sauce
¼ cup slice green onions with tops
4 teaspoons sesame seeds
1 tablespoon brown sugar
1 clove garlic, minced
⅛ teaspoon pepper
1½ pounds boneless pork loin,
　　cut into ¾-inch cubes
1 teaspoon cornstarch
1 green pepper, cut into
　　1-inch squares
12 medium-sized fresh mushrooms
6 wooden skewers

Combine pineapple juice, soy sauce, green onion, sesame seeds, brown sugar, garlic, and pepper in a large bowl; mix well. Set aside ⅛ cup marinade to baste skewers. Add pork to marinade; cover and refrigerate overnight, turning meat occasionally.

Soak skewers for 10 to 20 minutes in water. Drain the meat from the marinade. In a medium saucepan, blend 2 tablespoons of cold water and cornstarch. Add reserved marinade; cook and stir over medium heat until thickened. Alternate pepper, marinated meat, and mushrooms on 6 skewers. Place on a grill about 6 inches above medium coals. Cook 10 to 15 minutes, turning once. Brush with sauce occasionally.

Preparation time: 15 minutes
Marinating time: Overnight
Cooking time: 15 minutes

FRIED WON TONS

MAKES 30 WON TONS

Won Tons are thin wrappers stuffed with chopped meats and vegetables that may be deep fried, baked, or boiled. As an appetizer or in soup, won tons are best eaten hot.

½ pound ground lean pork
¾ cup minced carrot
½ cup minced green onion
½ cup finely chopped
  water chestnuts
3 cloves garlic, minced
2 tablespoons soy sauce
¼ teaspoon freshly ground
  black pepper
30 won ton wrappers
1 egg, separated
  Vegetable oil for frying
  Soy sauce (optional)
  Hot mustard (optional)

In a medium mixing bowl, combine the pork, carrot, onion, water chestnuts, garlic, soy sauce, and pepper. Spoon about 2 teaspoons of the filling onto the center of each won ton wrapper, allowing a ½-inch margin along each side. Moisten the inside edges of the wrapper with egg white and fold the two opposite edges together to form a triangle. Press the edges together to seal, pushing out as much air as possible.

In a large saucepan, heat oil 2 inches deep to 375° F. Lower won tons into the oil one at a time, keeping them separated. Fry for about 1 minute, or until the won tons are crisp and golden brown. Drain on paper towels. Serve hot with soy sauce or mustard.

Variations: For the pork filling, substitute 1 cup cooked and ground leg of lamb or ¼ pound ground pork and ¼ pound shelled and deveined shrimp.

Preparation time: 30 minutes
Cooking time: 15 minutes

BAKED WON TONS *Very Good*
WITH FRESH GINGER SAUCE

MAKES 30 WON TONS

Fresh Ginger Sauce
(recipe follows)
Won Ton filling (see
recipe above)
30 Won Ton wrappers

First prepare the Fresh Ginger Sauce and set aside. Prepare won ton filling (see recipe above). Then preheat the oven to 450° F. Grease a 10½ × 15½ × 1-inch baking sheet.

Fill and fold the won tons. In a small bowl, beat the reserved egg yolk with 2 teaspoons of water. Brush each won ton with the egg mixture and place on the prepared baking sheet. Bake about 5 minutes on each side or until golden brown, turning once during cooking. Serve warm with Fresh Ginger Sauce.

Preparation time: 30 minutes
Cooking time: 10 minutes

FRESH GINGER SAUCE *← Great!*

MAKES ABOUT 1 CUP

⅓ cup brown sugar
¼ cup white vinegar
2 tablespoon soy sauce
4 teaspoons cornstarch
1 tablespoon minced fresh ginger

In a small saucepan, bring ⅔ cup of water to a boil. Add to it the brown sugar, vinegar, soy sauce, cornstarch, and ginger and stir over high heat until the sauce boils and thickens. Strain the mixture through a fine-mesh sieve to catch all the ginger. Cool the sauce to room temperature before serving.

Preparation time: 3 minutes
Cooking time: 5 minutes

CLASSIC SOUPS

湯類

Chinese soups range from light to heavy, simple to complex and from hot and sour to sweet. They are prepared by cooking meat, poultry, or seafood, and vegetables in either stock or water. The lightest soups call for freshly boiled water poured over delicately seasoned minced greens. A light soup is designed to offset heavy, rich foods and must always be clear. Heavy, thick soups are simmered for a longer period of time which allows the ingredients to blend completely. Eaten with rice and a vegetable dish these soups provide a satisfying lunch. The most celebrated complex soups are the famous bird's nest soup and the shark's fin soup. These are served at formal Chinese dinners and banquets. Bird's nest soup is made from the gelatinous nest secreted by a swallow who builds her prized nest in tall trees. Shark's fin soup is made from the cartilage of the fin, which is tasteless when fresh, but translucent and tasty when dried. Hot and sour soup is one of the most delicious yet easily prepared soups in Chinese cuisine. Most likely originating in Sichuan province, it is found throughout China.

HOT AND SOUR SOUP WITH BEEF

MAKES 6 SERVINGS

1¾ pounds boneless beef chuck arm roast, thinly sliced
¼ cup soy sauce
4½ cups beef broth
¼ pound fresh mushrooms, thinly sliced, or ½ ounce dried shiitake mushrooms
1 8-ounce can sliced bamboo shoots, drained and cut into thin strips
3 tablespoon red wine vinegar
¼ teaspoon crushed red pepper pods
2 tablespoons cornstarch
1 egg, well beaten
4 ounces tofu, thinly sliced
2 teaspoons dark roasted sesame oil
2 green onions, thinly sliced on the diagonal

Cut the beef across the grain into thin, 2-inch long strips. Pour the soy sauce over the beef strips and stir to coat. In a Dutch oven, bring the beef broth to a boil. Add the beef mixture, reduce heat and cover the pan tightly. Cook slowly for 1 hour, or until the meat is tender.

To prepare dried shiitake mushrooms, soak them in warm water about 30 minutes. Save the stems and warm water to use for flavoring stock. Slice the mushrooms into strips and use as fresh mushrooms. Stir in the mushrooms, bamboo shoots, vinegar, and red pepper. Simmer, uncovered, for 10 minutes.

In a measuring cup, combine ½ cup cold water and cornstarch. Stir it into the soup and continue stirring until the soup is slightly thickened. Slowly pour the beaten egg into the soup in a thick stream, stirring constantly to make fine shreds. Add the tofu and heat through. Turn off heat and stir in sesame oil. Serve in warm bowls. Garnish with green onions.

Preparation time: 30 minutes
Cooking time: 1 hour 15 minutes

Hot and Sour Soup with Beef

TURKEY RICE SOUP

MAKES 6 SERVINGS

½ cup uncooked rice
7 cups turkey or chicken broth
2 cups coarsely chopped cooked turkey
1 cup diagonally sliced celery
2 medium carrots, cut in matchsticks
1 pound mixed vegetables
½ cup thinly sliced green onions
1 tablespoon soy sauce
2 tablespoons sherry
1½ teaspoons cornstarch

Combine rice and broth in a 4-quart saucepan and bring to a boil. Reduce heat, cover loosely and cook for 10 minutes. Add turkey, celery, and carrots. Simmer for 5 minutes. Stir in the mixed vegetables and green onions.

Blend soy sauce and sherry with cornstarch; add to broth. Simmer until soup is clear and slightly thickened, stirring occasionally. Ladle into soup bowls.

Preparation time: 5 minutes
Cooking time: 30 minutes

HOT AND SOUR SOUP WITH PORK

MAKE 6 SERVINGS *Very good (even w/ beef)*

6½ cups chicken broth
2 cups shredded Chinese cabbage
    (bok choy)
3 medium carrots, cut into
    matchsticks (about 2 cups)
2 cups thinly sliced fresh
    mushrooms
½ pound uncooked boneless pork,
    cut into matchsticks
1 tablespoon soy sauce
½ pound tofu, cut in ½-inch cubes
¼ cup cider vinegar
½ teaspoon freshly ground
    black pepper
¼ cup cornstarch
⅓ cup thinly sliced green onions

In a large saucepan, bring to a boil the broth, cabbage, carrots, mushrooms, pork, and soy sauce. Reduce heat to low and simmer, uncovered, for about 3 minutes. Add the tofu, vinegar, and pepper and return the soup to boiling.

Combine the cornstarch with ¼ cup warm water and stir it into the soup. Continue stirring and boil 1 minute longer, or until the soup thickens slightly. Serve in heated bowls. Top with sliced green onions.

Preparation time: 20 minutes
Cooking time: 20 minutes

HOT AND SOUR SCALLOP SOUP

MAKES 4 TO 6 SERVINGS

4 cups chicken broth
1 cup thinly sliced mushrooms
¼ cup sliced bamboo shoots
½ pound sea scallops or
    bay scallops
1 tablespoon soy sauce
¼ teaspoon white pepper*
2 tablespoons cornstarch
1 egg, beaten
3 tablespoons rice vinegar, or
    2 tablespoons white wine vinegar
⅓ cup thinly sliced green onion

NOTE: The spiciness of the soup may be increased by substituting Szechwan hot bean paste for the white pepper.

In a large saucepan, bring the chicken broth, mushrooms, and bamboo shoots to a boil. Reduce heat and simmer for 5 minutes.

Place scallops in a colander and rinse under cold, running water; pat dry with paper towels. When using sea scallops, remove the small tendon found on the side and slice horizontally into ¼-inch pieces. Add scallops, soy sauce, and white pepper to the saucepan and bring to a boil. When cooking scallops be sure not to overcook them. Cook scallops quickly over high heat for 2 to 4 minutes until they lose their translucent quality and become a flat white. If allowed to overcook, scallops become tough and rubbery.

Mix the cornstarch with 3 tablespoons of warm water. Add the cornstarch mixture to the saucepan, stirring constantly until the broth thickens. Continue to stir the soup briskly, gradually adding beaten egg in a thin stream.

Remove the saucepan from heat. Stir in vinegar. Pour into individual serving bowls. Sprinkle with green onion and serve immediately.

Preparation time: 7 minutes
Cooking time: 30 minutes

PORK AND VEGETABLE SOUP

MAKES 6 SERVINGS

1 tablespoon sesame oil
½ pound lean pork loin, cut into
  ¼ × 1-inch strips
⅛ teaspoon minced fresh ginger
6 cups chicken broth
½ cup thinly sliced carrots
¾ cup thinly sliced fresh
  mushrooms
¼ cup thinly sliced green onions
  Fresh Chinese parsley (cilantro)
  sprigs (optional)

In a wok or medium skillet, heat the sesame oil. Add pork and ginger; stir-fry over medium heat for 3 to 4 minutes. Drain pork and set aside.

In a 4-quart Dutch oven, bring 6 cups chicken broth to boil. Add carrots; reduce heat, cover and simmer for 10 minutes. Add mushrooms, green onion, and pork; simmer for 2 minutes.

Ladle the soup into individual serving bowls. Top each serving with a sprig of cilantro, if desired.

Preparation time: 20 minutes
Cooking time: 26 to 30 minutes

WON TON SOUP

MAKES 6 SERVINGS

30 filled won tons uncooked
   (recipe page 14)
6 cups chicken broth
1 cup finely chopped fresh spinach

In a large saucepan, bring 2 quarts of water to a boil and drop in the won tons. Return to a boil, reduce heat to medium-high and cook for 5 minutes or until tender. Drain.

Pour the broth into the saucepan and bring to a boil, add the spinach and won tons. Return to a boil. Serve immediately.

Preparation time: 20 minutes
Cooking time: 20 minutes

SALADS AND DRESSINGS

沙律

CHICKEN SALAD WITH GRAPES

MAKES 4 TO 6 SERVINGS

This refreshing salad combines three of the five basic flavors in Chinese cooking: salt, sweet, and fragrant.

4   *cups cooked chicken, shredded*
1   *head lettuce, thinly shredded*
4   *green onions, thinly sliced*
1   *bunch Chinese parsley (cilantro), chopped (reserve a few leaves for garnish)*
¼   *cup toasted sesame seeds*
1   *cup chopped peanuts or cashews, or slivered almonds*
2   *cups red or green grapes, halved or whole and seeded Lemon Dressing (recipe follows)*
3   *cups rice sticks*
1   *carrot, thinly sliced on diagonal Additional whole nuts (optional) Small clusters of grapes*

Mix together the chicken, lettuce, green onions, chopped Chinese parsley, sesame seeds, nuts, and grapes. Prepare the Lemon Dressing and pour over the chicken mixture; toss to coat completely.

In a wok, deep fry the rice sticks in sesame oil, a bunch at a time, until they become light and puffy. Do not let them burn. Drain on paper towels and place on 4 to 6 individual serving plates, forming a nest.

Spoon the chicken mixture over the rice sticks. Garnish with parsley leaves, a few carrot slices, and additional nuts, if desired. Place small clusters of grapes on each plate alongside the salads.

Preparation time: 5 minutes
Cooking time: 5 minutes

LEMON DRESSING

MAKES ½ CUP

½   *teaspoon dry mustard*
1   *teaspoon sugar*
3   *tablespoons lemon juice*
1   *clove garlic, minced*
1   *teaspoon soy sauce*
¼   *cup sesame oil*

Thoroughly blend all ingredients.

Preparation time: 5 minutes

At right: Chicken Salad with Grapes

EGG NOODLE SALAD

MAKES 4 TO 6 SERVINGS

1   2½-ounce package
      Chinese barbecue (Char Siu)
      seasoning mix*
½   pound pork shoulder
1   teaspoon sesame oil
2   eggs
1   teaspoon sesame oil
½   pound medium-sized shrimp
1   pound Chinese egg noodles,
      fresh or dried
1   teaspoon sesame oil
2   cups chicken stock
2   tablespoons soy sauce
1   tablespoon peanut butter
1   tablespoon rice vinegar
½   teaspoon salt
3   tablespoons sugar
5   drops chili oil
5   drops roasted sesame seed oil
1   cucumber, unpeeled, and cut
      into matchsticks
4   green onions, green tops only
½   cup sliced almonds, toasted

Prepare the Chinese barbecue seasoning mix according to package directions. Cut the pork shoulder into 2 × 4-inch pieces. Pour seasoning marinade over pork, cover and refrigerate for 1 hour. Remove the pork from the marinade and roast at 350° F for 40 minutes, or until done. Cool and slice into bite-sized pieces.

Make egg threads by cooking a two-egg omelet in 1 teaspoon of sesame oil. Slice the omelet into thin strips ¼-inch wide.

Rinse and devein the shrimp. Sauté the shrimp in 1 teaspoon vegetable oil until they turn pink. Chill.

Cook the noodles according to packaged directions. Rinse in cold water and drain well. Toss the noodles with sesame oil. Cover and chill for 2 hours.

In a small saucepan, combine the chicken stock, soy sauce, peanut butter, vinegar, salt, sugar, chili oil, and sesame oil. Heat until well blended and let cool at room temperature.

Place the chilled noodles on a large, deep platter. Garnish with the green onions. Serve barbecued pork, shrimp, cucumber, and almonds on the side. Spoon sauce over the salad.

Preparation time: 15 minutes
Marinating time: 1 hour
Cooking time: 45 minutes
Chilling time: 2 hours

NOTE: Available at most Asian specialty markets.

SPICY PEANUT CHICKEN SALAD

MAKES 4 SERVINGS

2   cups cooked chicken, shredded
1   cucumber, pared, seeded
      and sliced
1   green onion, thinly sliced
1   teaspoon ground ginger
1   clove garlic, minced
⅓   cup creamy peanut butter
2   tablespoons soy sauce
1½ tablespoons red wine vinegar
1   tablespoon peanut oil
1   teaspoon sugar
½   teaspoon hot pepper sauce
      Watercress
2   tablespoons salted peanuts,
      chopped

In a medium bowl, mix together the chicken, cucumber, green onion, ginger, and garlic. In a small bowl, combine the peanut butter, soy sauce, vinegar, oil, sugar, hot pepper sauce, and 3 tablespoons of water. Pour sauce over the chicken mixture. Toss gently to coat. Make a bed of watercress on each plate. Top with chicken salad. Garnish with chopped peanuts. Serve hot or cold.

Preparation time: 5 minutes

SHANGHAI BEEF SALAD

MAKES 6 SERVINGS

DRESSING

1¾	cups peanut oil
⅞	cup rice vinegar
7	tablespoons lemon juice
⅞	cup soy sauce
7	tablespoons sesame oil
2	teaspoons minced garlic
1	tablespoon chopped Chinese parsley (cilantro)
½	teaspoon sugar

SALAD

1	pound beef flank steak
12	curly lettuce leaves
¼	cup canned fried rice noodles
¼	pound fresh mushrooms, thinly sliced
1	cup broccoli florets, steamed
2	tomatoes, sliced
1	green pepper, thinly sliced
1	red bell pepper, thinly sliced
2	tablespoons sesame seeds, toasted
6	Chinese parsley (cilantro) sprigs

In a bowl, combine dressing ingredients. Whisk to blend; set aside.

Grill the flank steak to desired doneness. Cut into thin slices.

For each salad serving, line a salad plate with lettuce leaves. Divide the noodles, beef, mushrooms, broccoli, tomatoes, and peppers among the lettuce leaves. Sprinkle the salads with sesame seeds and garnish with a cilantro sprig. Serve with dressing.

Preparation time: 10 minutes
Cooking time: 15 minutes

CRUNCHY PORK SALAD

MAKES 4 SERVINGS

4	slices bacon
¾	pound pork, cooked and cubed
6	cups torn iceberg lettuce
1	8-ounce can sliced water chestnuts, drained
½	cup sliced green onions
3	tablespoons soy sauce
2	tablespoons honey
1	tablespoon catsup
1	teaspoon dry mustard
1	3-ounce can chow mein noodles

In a wok or large skillet, cook the bacon until crisp. Let drain on paper towels and crumble; set aside.

In a large bowl, combine the crumbled bacon, pork, lettuce, water chestnuts, and green onions. Cover and refrigerate 2 to 3 hours.

To prepare the dressing, in a small bowl combine the soy sauce, honey, catsup, and dry mustard. Cover and shake well. Chill.

To serve, add the dressing and chow mein noodles to the salad, tossing lightly to coat.

Preparation time: 5 minutes
Cooking time: 3 minutes
Chilling time: 2 to 3 hours

MEATS AND POULTRY

肉類及雞類

CURRIED BEEF STIR-FRY

MAKES 4 TO 5 SERVINGS

1 pound Chinese egg noodles,
  fresh or dried
2 tablespoons soy sauce
2 tablespoons peanut oil
½ pound flank steak or
  boneless sirloin
2 teaspoons cornstarch
1 tablespoon soy sauce
1 teaspoon dry sherry
½ teaspoon salt
2 cloves garlic, minced
  Curry Sauce (recipe follows)
2 tablespoons peanut oil
2 stalks celery, sliced diagonally
  into ¼-inch pieces
1 yellow onion, cut into
  bite-sized pieces
1 bell pepper, cut into
  bite-sized pieces
1 tomato, cut into 12 wedges

Cook the noodles in boiling water according to package directions. Run cold water over noodles to cool quickly; drain thoroughly. Add soy sauce and peanut oil and mix well. Divide the noodles between 2 platters. Allow to stand uncovered at room temperature for 2 hours to dry.

Slice the steak diagonally into very thin slices. In a bowl, mix the cornstarch, soy sauce, dry sherry, salt, and garlic. Sprinkle on steak and set aside. Prepare Curry Sauce and set aside.

In a wok or skillet with a nonstick coating, heat 2 tablespoons of the peanut oil over medium heat. Add one platter of noodles and fry pancake style until the noodles are light brown on each side. Repeat with the other platter of noodles. Remove from skillet and keep warm.

Add the remaining 2 tablespoons of oil to the skillet. Add celery, onion, and bell pepper; stir-fry 2 minutes and remove. To stir-fry beef mixture, keep the heat on high and add more oil if necessary. Add small amounts of the beef at a time. When beef is cooked, return the vegetables to the skillet and add tomatoes and curry sauce. Stir-fry until sauce thickens and turns color. Serve immediately over the hot noodles.

Preparation time: 20 minutes
Drying time: 2 hours
Cooking time: 10 to 12 minutes

CURRY SAUCE

½ cup chicken stock
1 tablespoon Worcestershire sauce
3 tablespoons catsup
1 teaspoon curry powder
1 tablespoon cornstarch
1 tablespoon soy sauce

In a small bowl, combine all the ingredients; set aside.

Quick Szechwan Steaks

QUICK SZECHWAN STEAKS

MAKES 4 SERVINGS

Szechwan Steaks updates the classic steak 'au poivre' with an Asian flair, using either naturally lean beef eye round steaks or beef tenderloin steaks.

4	*beef eye round steaks or beef tenderloin steaks, cut 1 inch thick (approximately 1 pound)*
½ to 1	*teaspoon crushed Szechwan or black peppercorns*
½	*cup beef broth*
1	*tablespoon dry sherry*
½	*teaspoon soy sauce*

Press the pepper onto both sides of each beef steak. Heat a wok or heavy nonstick skillet over medium heat. Add the steaks and panbroil for 8 to 10 minutes, to desired doneness, turning once. Remove the steaks from the skillet and keep warm.

Add the beef broth, sherry, and soy sauce to the pan; cook and stir until the meat juices attached to the pan are dissolved. Continue cooking for 2 to 3 minutes, or until the liquid is slightly reduced.

Carve each steak into ¼-inch slices and spoon sauce over.

Preparation time: 5 minutes
Cooking time: 10 to 13 minutes

BEIJING BEEF

MAKES 6 SERVINGS

1½   pounds flank steak or top round
     steak, thinly sliced across the
     grain, 1-inch wide
½   cup soy sauce
1   tablespoon grated fresh ginger
1   tablespoon minced garlic
¼   cup peanut oil
2   tablespoons sesame oil
¾   pound asparagus, sliced
     diagonally into 1-inch pieces
½   cup thinly sliced red bell pepper
½   teaspoon cornstarch
¾   pound Napa cabbage, shredded
⅓   pound bok choy leaves,
     steamed (optional)
1   tablespoon toasted
     sesame seeds

Toss the steak, soy sauce, ginger, and garlic in a medium-sized bowl. Set aside.

Heat 2 tablespoons of the peanut oil and 1 tablespoon sesame oil in a wok or skillet. Add steak; stir-fry over high heat until beef loses its red color.

Add asparagus and red bell pepper; stir-fry until vegetables are tender crisp.

Dissolve cornstarch in 2 teaspoons water. Stir into beef mixture, tossing to thicken.

To serve, arrange ¼ cup of the cabbage and 2 tablespoons of the bok choy on each serving plate. Top with beef mixture and sprinkle with sesame seeds.

Preparation time: 15 minutes
Cooking time: 5 minutes

BEEF AND VEGETABLES IN OYSTER SAUCE

MAKES 4 SERVINGS

¾   pound beef sirloin,
     sliced into ⅛-inch strips
     Freshly ground black pepper
3   tablespoons soy sauce
1   clove garlic, minced
2   bok choy, ribs and leaves
1   large red bell pepper,
     thinly sliced
1   medium yellow onion,
     thinly sliced
½   pound fresh mushrooms,
     thinly sliced
1   tablespoon cornstarch
2   tablespoons oyster sauce
2   tablespoons peanut oil
     Hot cooked rice or crispy
     chow mein noodles

Season beef strips with black pepper. In a shallow dish, combine the beef, soy sauce, garlic, and 3 tablespoons of water. Cover and refrigerate for at least 1 hour.

Cut the bok choy ribs diagonally into ½-inch pieces; measure 1 cup. Shred the bok choy leaves. Place all the vegetables near the wok or skillet, in their order of use.

Drain the marinade from the beef and discard. Combine ⅓ cup water, cornstarch, and oyster sauce in a cup; blend until smooth. Set aside.

In a wok or large skillet, heat the oil. When the oil is hot, add beef strips and stir-fry over medium-high heat 3 to 4 minutes, or until beef loses its pink color. Remove the beef from the skillet or push to one side of the wok. Add the bok choy ribs, bell pepper, and onion; stir-fry for about 2 minutes. Add mushrooms; stir-fry for about 2 minutes. Add bok choy leaves, cooked beef, and sauce. Stir to coat ingredients evenly with sauce. Heat just until the leaves wilt and the sauce is thickened. Serve immediately with hot steamed rice or crispy chow mein noodles.

Preparation time: 15 minutes
Marinating time: 1 hour
Cooking time: 25 minutes

BEEF AND PEPPERS CANTONESE

MAKES 2 SERVINGS

½ pound beef top round or boneless sirloin steak, cut 1-inch thick, or beef flank steak
2 tablespoons dry sherry
2 tablespoons soy sauce
2 teaspoons cornstarch
1½ teaspoons dark roasted sesame oil
1 teaspoon sugar
2 tablespoons peanut, safflower or corn oil
1 large red or green bell pepper, cut into ¾-inch chunks
1 teaspoon minced fresh ginger
1 tablespoon minced green onion

Cut the steak across the grain into ⅛-inch strips.

In a bowl, combine ½ cup of water, sherry, soy sauce, cornstarch, sesame oil, and sugar; mix well. Place beef and ⅓ cup of the sauce mixture in a shallow dish, turning the meat to coat. Cover and refrigerate for 30 minutes, turning the meat at least once. Reserve remaining sauce mixture.

Heat 1 tablespoon of the oil in a wok or nonstick skillet over medium-high heat until hot. Remove the beef from marinade; discard marinade. Stir-fry the beef for about 1½ minutes, or until no longer pink. Remove beef from skillet; set aside.

Add the remaining 1 tablespoon of oil to skillet; heat until hot. Add peppers and ginger; stir-fry over medium-high heat 2 to 3 minutes, or until the peppers are crisp-tender. Add the reserved sauce mixture and stir until the sauce is slightly thickened. Add the reserved beef; toss lightly to coat. Sprinkle with green onions and serve immediately. This recipe can be easily doubled.

Preparation time: 25 minutes
Marinating time: 30 minutes
Cooking time: 9 to 10 minutes

MANDARIN BEEF

MAKES 4 SERVINGS

1 pound beef flank steak
3 tablespoons soy sauce
2 tablespoons vegetable oil
1 tablespoon cornstarch
1 tablespoon brown sugar
¼ pound green beans, cut diagonally into 2-inch pieces
1 10-ounce package frozen asparagus, thawed and cut diagonally into 2-inch pieces, or 12 ounces fresh asparagus, cut diagonally into 2-inch pieces and blanched for 2 minutes
¼ pound mushrooms, thinly sliced
2 tablespoons dry sherry
6 green onions, cut into 2-inch slivers
½ teaspoon dark roasted sesame oil

Cut beef flank steak lengthwise in half. Cut steak across the grain into ⅛-inch thick strips. In a bowl, combine 1 tablespoon of the soy sauce, 1 teaspoon of the vegetable oil, cornstarch, and 1 teaspoon of the brown sugar. Pour over beef strips, cover and marinate for 30 minutes.

Heat a wok or nonstick skillet over medium heat. Add the remaining oil. Stir-fry the green beans for 3 to 4 minutes. Add the asparagus and mushrooms and stir-fry 2 minutes longer. Transfer the vegetables to a warm platter.

In a bowl, combine the sherry, the remaining 2 tablespoons of soy sauce and 1 teaspoon of brown sugar; set aside.

Stir-fry beef one-third at a time for 2 to 3 minutes; set aside. Return the beef, vegetables, and sherry mixture to the skillet and heat through. Stir in green onion. Add sesame oil and stir. Serve immediately.

Preparation time: 20 minutes
Marinating time: 30 minutes
Cooking time: 25 minutes

MOO SHOO BEEF WITH MANDARIN PANCAKES

MAKES 12 FILLED PANCAKES

This recipe shows how to make Chinese pancakes from scratch. To save time, you may substitute flour tortillas.

MANDARIN PANCAKES

- 1 cup plus 2 tablespoons all-purpose flour
- ½ cup boiling water
  Sesame oil

Mix flour and water with a fork until the dough holds together. Turn out onto a lightly floured surface and knead 8 minutes, or until the dough is smooth. Shape the dough into a roll 12 inches long. Cut the roll into 12 1-inch slices. Cover the slices with plastic wrap to keep from drying out.

Shape two of the dough pieces into balls; flatten slightly. Roll each ball into a 4- to 5-inch circle on a lightly floured surface. Brush one pancake lightly with oil and top with the second pancake. Roll double pancake into an 8-inch circle on a lightly floured surface.

Heat a small ungreased skillet 1 minute over high heat. Reduce the heat to medium and cook the pancake 1 to 2 minutes, turning once. The pancake should be blistered with small air pockets and appear parchment-colored. Separate into 2 pancakes immediately and fold each pancake into fourths; set aside. Repeat this process to make 12 pancakes.

Preparation time: 40 minutes
Cooking time: 16 to 22 minutes

MOO SHOO BEEF

- 1½ pounds beef flank steak
- 2 tablespoons hoisin sauce
- 2 tablespoons soy sauce
- 1 clove garlic, minced
- 2 tablespoons sesame oil
- 1 egg, beaten
- ¼ teaspoon salt
- 1 cup thinly sliced mushrooms
- ½ cup coarsely chopped red pepper
- 14 ounces bean sprouts, canned or fresh
- 1 8-ounce can bamboo shoots, drained and thinly sliced
- 1 tablespoon cornstarch
- ⅔ cup sliced green onion
- ½ cup prepared plum sauce

Cut the steak in half lengthwise and slice each half diagonally across the grain into very thin slices. While cutting, knife should be almost parallel to the cutting surface. Cut slices with the grain into thin strips and place strips in a shallow baking dish.

In a bowl, combine 2 tablespoons of water, hoisin sauce, soy sauce, and garlic; pour over the beef strips. Cover and marinate in the refrigerator for 30 minutes.

In a wok or large skillet, heat 1 tablespoon of the sesame oil over medium heat. In a bowl, combine the egg and salt; pour into the wok and rotate to coat the bottom. (Do not rotate the skillet.) Fry egg for 1 minute, or until set. Remove from wok and coarsely chop; set aside.

Heat the remaining oil and stir-fry the beef one-third at a time for 2 to 3 minutes. Remove beef from pan; set aside. Stir-fry the mushrooms and red pepper 2 minutes. Add bean sprouts and bamboo shoots and continue cooking for 1 minute longer.

Heat pancakes before serving by placing on a rack in a steamer, covering and steaming for 10 minutes.

In a cup, combine ¼ cup water and the cornstarch to make a smooth paste. Add to vegetables in the wok and cook until sauce is thickened, stirring occasionally. Stir in beef strips, cooked egg, and green onion and heat through.

To serve, brush one side of each Mandarin Pancake lightly with plum sauce. Spoon about ½ cup of the beef mixture onto the center of each pancake. Fold the two opposite sides over the filling, overlapping the edges about ½ inch from the center. Fold one unfolded edge over the folded sides to form a pocket.

Preparation time: 45 minutes
Marinating time: 30 minutes
Cooking time: 18 to 20 minutes

Moo Shoo Beef with Mandarin Pancakes

ORANGE BARBECUE RIBS

MAKES 6 SERVINGS

2   pounds well-trimmed beef short
    ribs, cut ⅜ to ½-inch thick
⅓   cup orange juice
3   tablespoons hoisin sauce
2   tablespoons minced green onion
2   tablespoons rice wine vinegar or
    wine vinegar
1   tablespoon soy sauce
1   clove garlic, minced
½   teaspoon crushed red
    pepper pods

Combine the orange juice concentrate, hoisin sauce, onion, vinegar, soy sauce, garlic, and pepper pods for a marinade. Reserve 3 tablespoons of the marinade, covered, in the refrigerator to use during cooking as a basting sauce. Place the short ribs in a bowl and pour marinade over, turning to coat the meat. Cover and refrigerate for 6 to 8 hours, or overnight, turning occasionally.

Remove ribs from marinade; discard marinade. Place ribs on a grill over medium coals. Grill 10 to 12 minutes, turning once and brushing with reserved marinade before turning.

Preparation time: 15 minutes
Marinating time: 6 to 8 hours,
*   or overnight*
Cooking time: 10 to 12 minutes

SZECHWAN BEEF STIR-FR

MAKES 4 SERVINGS

1   pound beef flank steak, sliced
    into ⅛-inch strips
2   tablespoons soy sauce
4   teaspoons dark roasted
    sesame oil
½   teaspoon sugar
1   teaspoon cornstarch
2   cloves garlic, crushed
1   tablespoon minced fresh ginger
¼   teaspoon crushed red
    pepper pods
1   small red bell pepper,
    cut into 1-inch pieces
1   8-ounce package frozen
    baby corn, thawed

In a bowl, combine the soy sauce, 2 teaspoons of the oil, sugar, and cornstarch; add the beef strips.

Heat the remaining 2 teaspoons of the sesame oil in a wok or large skillet over medium-high heat. Add the garlic, ginger, and pepper pods; stir-fry 30 seconds. Add the bell pepper and corn; stir-fry 1½ minutes. Remove the vegetables.

Stir-fry half the beef strips at one time for 2 to 3 minutes. Return the vegetables to the skillet and heat through.

Preparation time: 20 minutes
Cooking time: 6 to 8 minutes

HONEY-GLAZED VEAL RIBLETS

MAKES 4 SERVINGS

2½ to 3   pounds veal riblets
2   cups orange juice
½   cup dry white wine
2   tablespoons soy sauce
1   tablespoon honey
1   clove garlic, minced
2   teaspoons grated
    fresh ginger
½   teaspoon fresh shredded
    orange peel
1¼   teaspoons cornstarch
    Chopped green onion

In a large wok or Dutch oven, combine the veal riblets, 1½ cups of the orange juice, and wine. Bring to a boil. Reduce heat to low. Cover tightly and simmer for 45 minutes, turning the riblets occasionally.

Meanwhile, combine the remaining orange juice, soy sauce, honey, garlic, ginger, and orange peel in a small saucepan. Dissolve the cornstarch in 1 tablespoon of cold water. Add the cornstarch mixture to the saucepan; mix well. Bring the glaze to a boil over medium-high heat, stirring constantly. Cook and stir 1 more minute. Remove from heat; set aside.

Remove the cooked riblets from the liquid; let cool for 15 minutes. Place the riblets on a grill over medium coals; brush with honey glaze. Or, in an oven, broil 4 inches from heat, turning frequently and brushing with glaze, for about 12 minutes. Transfer the riblets to a platter and sprinkle with green onion.

Preparation time: 15 minutes
Cooking time: 1 hour 15 minutes

SESAME VEAL KABOBS

MAKES 4 SERVINGS

1 pound veal leg cutlets,
  cut ¼-inch thick
⅓ cup dry white wine
2 tablespoons thinly sliced
  green onion
2 teaspoons dark roasted sesame
  oil
1 teaspoon grated fresh ginger
2 cloves garlic, minced
¼ teaspoon salt
8 wooden skewers

Cut the veal leg cutlets into 1-inch wide strips. Combine the wine, green onion, sesame oil, ginger, garlic, and salt in a medium-sized bowl. Add the veal strips, turning to coat. Cover the bowl and marinate in the refrigerator for 30 minutes to 2 hours, turning occasionally.

Soak skewers in water for 10 to 20 minutes. Remove the veal from the marinade. Weaving them back and forth, thread an equal amount of veal strips on each skewer, but do not crowd. Place the kabobs on a grill 4 to 5 inches above medium-hot coals. Grill for 4 to 5 minutes, turning once.

Kabobs may also be oven broiled. Place the kabobs on the rack of a broiler pan, about 4 inches from the heat. Broil 3 to 5 minutes, or until cooked through, turning once.

Preparation time: 15 minutes
Marinating time: 30 minutes to 2 hours
Cooking time: 4 to 5 minutes

SPICY LAMB STIR-FRY

Very Good.
Can use top
sirloin.

Serves 4-5.

MAKES 4 SERVINGS

1 pound boneless lamb leg, cut
  into 3 × 1 × ⅛-inch strips
4 tablespoons lemon juice
4 tablespoons soy sauce
2 tablespoons honey
3 teaspoons minced fresh ginger,
  or ½ teaspoon ground ginger
4 cloves garlic, minced
½ teaspoon red pepper flakes
2 teaspoons cornstarch
2 teaspoons vegetable oil
1 tablespoon sesame or
  vegetable oil
4 cups of sliced vegetables, such as
  green onions, mushrooms, red or
  green bell peppers, zucchini or
  yellow squash, carrots, celery,
  trimmed snow peas, water
  chestnuts, cauliflower or
  broccoli florets
  Hot cooked rice (optional)

In a medium bowl, combine the lemon juice, soy sauce, honey, ginger, garlic, and red pepper flakes. Reserve half of the marinade to use in the sauce. Add the lamb strips to the bowl; cover and refrigerate for at least 2 hours.

In a small bowl, blend the cornstarch with 1 tablespoon of water until smooth; set aside.

Place a wok or heavy skillet over high heat until hot. Add vegetable oil, swirling to coat sides. Add sesame oil and heat over high heat. Drain the lamb and discard the marinade. Add the lamb and the reserved marinade to the wok and stir-fry until the lamb is no longer pink, about 3 to 4 minutes. Transfer the cooked lamb to a bowl using a slotted spoon.

Add the sliced vegetables to the wok. Stir-fry until the sauce turns translucent, about 30 to 60 seconds. Return the lamb to the wok; toss with vegetables and heat through. Serve immediately over hot rice, if desired.

Preparation time: 20 minutes
Marinating time: 2 hours
Cooking time: 7 minutes

SWEET AND SOUR LAMB STIR-FRY

MAKES 6 SERVINGS

3   tablespoons red wine
3   tablespoons soy sauce
1   tablespoon vegetable oil
1   pound shoulder or leg of lamb,
    cut in ⅛-inch strips
3   green onions and tops,
    sliced diagonally
2   stalks celery, sliced diagonally
1   medium red or green bell
    pepper, cut in thin strips
½   pound fresh mushrooms,
    thinly sliced
1   medium carrot, thinly sliced
¼   teaspoon garlic powder
1½ tablespoons cornstarch
½   teaspoon ground ginger
6   tablespoons pineapple juice,
    reserved from pineapple chunks
3   tablespoons soy sauce
2   tablespoons apple cider vinegar
1   10½-ounce can pineapple chunks
    packed in heavy syrup
½   cup chopped cashews
1   2-ounce jar sliced pimentos
    Hot cooked rice (optional)
    Soy sauce

Combine the red wine and 3 table-spoons of soy sauce; pour over lamb strips, cover and refrigerate for 2 hours.

Heat oil in a wok or skillet. Add marinated lamb strips and brown for 2 to 3 minutes. Add the green onions, celery, bell pepper, mushrooms, and carrot; stir-fry another 2 minutes. Remove the lamb mixture; set aside. Drain pineapple and reserve juice.

In a small bowl, combine the garlic powder, cornstarch, ginger, pine-apple juice, soy sauce, and cider vine-gar. Stir until completely blended. Add the sauce to the wok and stir constantly until thickened.

Return the lamb mixture to the wok and add the remaining ingredients. Stir-fry for 1 minute, allowing the sauce to coat the lamb mixture com-pletely. Serve with hot rice and soy sauce.

Preparation time: 20 minutes
Marinating time: 2 hours
Cooking time: 7 to 10 minutes

Sweet and Sour Lamb Stir-fry

TRADITIONAL LAMB STIR-FRY

MAKES 4 SERVINGS

½ cup soy sauce
2 tablespoons red wine
½ teaspoon garlic powder
¼ teaspoon ground ginger
1 tablespoon cornstarch
¼ teaspoon freshly ground
   black pepper
⅛ teaspoon cayenne pepper
3 tablespoons sesame oil
1 pound lean lamb leg, cut into
   3 × 1-inch strips
3 carrots, cut into matchsticks
2 stalks celery, sliced diagonally
1 cup thinly sliced mushrooms
1 6-ounce package frozen
   pea pods, thawed
3 cups shredded cabbage
1 8-ounce can sliced water
   chestnuts, drained
6 green onions, sliced diagonally
1 2-ounce can diced pimento,
   drained
1 tablespoon sesame seeds,
   toasted
   Hot cooked rice (optional)

In a small bowl, combine the soy sauce, red wine, garlic powder, ground ginger, cornstarch, pepper, and cayenne; set aside.

Add the sesame oil to the wok or skillet. When hot, add the lamb strips and stir-fry for 2 minutes. Add the carrots, celery and mushrooms; stir-fry with the lamb for 2 minutes. Remove the lamb and vegetables from the wok and keep warm.

Add the soy sauce mixture to the wok; stir until the mixture begins to thicken. Immediately return the lamb and cooked vegetables to the wok. Add the pea pods, cabbage, chestnuts, onions, and pimento; stir-fry for 2 minutes. Just before serving, sprinkle the lamb with the toasted sesame seeds. Serve with hot cooked rice.

Preparation time: 20 minutes
Cooking time: 10 minutes

Fresh cabbage at the market

MANDARIN LAMB WITH NOODLES

MAKES 4 SERVINGS

1 tablespoon cooking oil
2 cloves garlic, minced
1 pound boneless leg or shoulder
   of lamb, cut into ⅛-inch strips
1 3-ounce package beef flavor
   Ramen noodles
1 small zucchini or yellow squash,
   cut in half and sliced diagonally
1 carrot, thinly sliced
½ medium red bell pepper, cut in
   ⅛-inch strips
2 stalks celery, thinly sliced
¼ cup sweet and sour sauce
½ cup mandarin orange sections
¼ cup coarsely chopped almonds
   or peanuts

In a wok or large skillet, heat the oil and garlic until a light haze forms over it. Add the lamb strips and stir-fry about 3 minutes, or until the lamb is no longer pink. Remove the lamb from the skillet and set aside.

Break up the dry noodles and place them in the skillet with 1 cup of water, the flavor packet, and the squash, carrot, bell pepper, and celery. Bring the noodle mixture to a boil, stirring occasionally. Reduce heat, cover and simmer for 3 to 5 minutes, or until the vegetables are crisp-tender. Stir in the cooked lamb, sweet and sour sauce, and orange sections; heat through. To serve, top with nuts.

Preparation time: 10 minutes
Cooking time: 15 minutes

SWEET AND SOUR PORK

MAKES 4 SERVINGS

This Cantonese standard offers an interesting combination of flavors from the sweet and sour sauce to the tender pork, green peppers, and pineapple chunks.

1   pound boneless pork loin
1   tablespoon vegetable oil
1   medium green pepper,
     cut into 1-inch pieces
1   medium yellow onion,
     cut into thin wedges
1   15¼-ounce can pineapple chunks
     in juice
¼   cup firmly packed brown sugar
¼   cup white wine vinegar
2   tablespoons cornstarch
2   tablespoons soy sauce
     Hot cooked rice (optional)

Cut the pork across the grain into 2½ × 2¼-inch strips; set aside.

Heat a wok or large skillet over high heat; add oil. Stir-fry the green pepper and onion in the hot oil for 2 to 3 minutes, or until crisp-tender. Remove from wok and set aside. Add more oil, if necessary. Add half the pork to wok; stir-fry until browned. Remove pork; stir-fry the remaining pork. Return all the pork to wok; keep warm.

Drain the pineapple, reserving the juice. In a small saucepan, combine the juice, brown sugar, vinegar, cornstarch, and soy sauce. Bring to a boil and cook for about 1 minute, or until thickened, stirring constantly.

Return the green pepper and onion to the wok. Stir in the pineapple and the thickened pineapple juice mixture. Cook and stir until heated through. Serve with hot cooked rice, if desired.

Preparation time: 20 minutes
Cooking time: 15 minutes

SESAME PORK WITH BROCCOLI

MAKES 6 SERVINGS

1¾   cup chicken broth
2   tablespoons cornstarch
1   teaspoon soy sauce
4   green onions, finely diced,
     including green tops
1   pound pork tenderloin
1   teaspoon vegetable oil
1   clove garlic, minced
1½   pounds fresh broccoli, cut into
     bite-sized pieces (about 7 cups)
2   tablespoons sliced pimento,
     drained
2   tablespoons sesame seed,
     lightly toasted

In a small bowl, combine the chicken broth, cornstarch, and soy sauce; blend well. Stir in the green onions; set aside.

Cut pork tenderloin lengthwise into quarters; cut each quarter into bite-sized pieces. Heat oil in a wok or nonstick skillet over medium-high heat. Add the pork and garlic; stir-fry for 3 to 4 minutes, or until the pork is tender. Remove pork; keep warm.

Add broccoli and broth mixture to the skillet. Cover and simmer over low heat for 8 minutes. Add the cooked pork and pimento. Cook just until the mixture is hot, stirring frequently. Sprinkle with toasted sesame seed. Serve immediately.

Preparation time: 20 minutes
Cooking time: 15 to 20 minutes

BAKED SPARERIBS

MAKES 6 SERVINGS

6   pounds pork spareribs
½   cup hoisin sauce
6   tablespoons dry sherry
4   tablespoons honey
4   tablespoons soy sauce
4   cloves garlic, minced

Cut the spareribs into serving-size portions; set aside

Place a large plastic bag in a large bowl. In the bag, combine the remaining ingredients with ¼ cup water; mix well. Reserve half the marinade to use as a basting sauce. Add the ribs and close the bag tightly. Refrigerate for 6 hours or overnight, turning bag several times to distribute the marinade.

Drain the ribs, discarding the marinade. Place the ribs in a shallow roasting pan. Cover with foil and bake in a 350° F oven for 1½ hours. Uncover the ribs and brush with the reserved marinade. Bake, uncovered for 30 minutes longer, or until done.

Preparation time: 10 minutes
Marinating time: 6 hours to overnight
Cooking time: 2 hours

GINGER PORK WITH PEANUT SAUCE

MAKES 4 SERVINGS

1   pound pork tenderloin
1   3-ounce package pork-flavored
    Ramen noodles
2   teaspoons vegetable oil
½   teaspoon dry red pepper flakes
1   teaspoon fresh ginger,
    cut into matchsticks
¼   cup peanut butter
2   tablespoons soy sauce
2   cups torn spinach,
    washed and drained
¼   cup sliced green onions

Cut the pork tenderloin into ¼-inch slices, trimming as necessary; cut each slice in half.

Cook the noodles according to package directions. Drain and keep warm. Reserve cooking water.

Heat oil in a skillet; add pork, red pepper flakes, and ginger. Cook and stir until pork is done, about 4 to 5 minutes. Remove the pork and keep warm. Discard the cooking oil.

Blend peanut butter, ½ cup of the reserved cooking water, and soy sauce; heat and stir until hot, adding more cooking water if needed.

Toss the cooked pork, noodles, spinach, and green onions with the peanut sauce. Serve immediately.

Preparation time: 5 minutes
Cooking time: 20 minutes

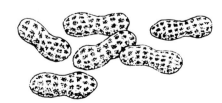

Ginger Pork and Melon

GINGER PORK AND MELON

MAKES 4 SERVINGS

1 tablespoon vegetable oil
1 pound fresh ham, cubed
½ yellow onion, thinly sliced
1 clove garlic, minced
1 tablespoon grated fresh ginger,
  or 1 teaspoon dry ginger
2 tablespoons soy sauce
¼ cup dry sherry
2 tablespoons wine vinegar
1 tablespoon cornstarch
3 cups cubed melon (cantaloupe
  or honeydew)
½ cup pickled watermelon rind,
  diced

Heat oil in a wok or heavy skillet over medium-high heat. Brown pork cubes, stirring, until lightly browned, about 4 to 5 minutes. Stir in the onion, garlic, and ginger; cook and stir for 2 to 3 minutes.

In a bowl, mix together the soy sauce, sherry, vinegar, and cornstarch. Add soy mixture to skillet. Cook and stir until the sauce thickens. Stir in the melon and watermelon rind. Heat through.

Preparation time: 20 minutes
Cooking time: 10 minutes

MANDARIN PORK

MAKES 4 SERVINGS

1   pound pork tenderloin
1   tablespoon grated orange rind
¾   cup orange juice
1   tablespoon cornstarch
1   tablespoon soy sauce
⅓   cup corn syrup
¼   teaspoon ground ginger
2   teaspoons vegetable oil
2   large carrots, peeled and
     sliced diagonally
2   stalks celery, peeled and
     sliced diagonally
½   cup cashews
     Hot cooked rice (optional)

Cut the pork tenderloin into thin strips; set aside.

In a small bowl, combine the orange rind, orange juice, cornstarch, soy sauce, corn syrup, and ginger, stirring well.

Heat 1 teaspoon of the oil in a wok or nonstick skillet over medium heat. Add the carrots and celery and stir-fry about 3 minutes. Remove the vegetables; set aside.

Pour the remaining 1 tablespoon of oil into the skillet. Add the pork; stir-fry for about 3 minutes. Return the vegetables to the skillet, add the orange juice mixture and cashews. Cook, stirring constantly, over medium-high heat, until thickened. Serve over rice, if desired.

Preparation time: 20 minutes
Cooking time: 15 minutes

VEGETABLE PORK STIR-FRY

MAKES 6 SERVINGS

1   tablespoon peanut oil
¾   pound pork tenderloin,
       cut into ⅛-inch strips
1½   cups thinly sliced mushrooms
1   green pepper, cut into strips
1   zucchini, thinly sliced
2   ribs celery, diagonally sliced
1   cup thinly sliced carrots
1   clove garlic, minced
1   cup chicken broth
2   tablespoons soy sauce
1½   tablespoons cornstarch

Add oil to a hot wok or skillet. Brown the pork strips in hot oil over medium-high heat. Push meat to the side of the wok. Add mushrooms, pepper, zucchini, celery, carrots, and garlic; stir-fry for 3 minutes. In a small bowl, combine broth, soy sauce, and cornstarch; add to wok and cook until thickened. Serve immediately.

Preparation time: 8 minutes
Cooking time: 8 to 10 minutes

Restaurant workers in the city of Xi'an mixing cooking oil

SIMPLE ROAST DUCK

MAKES 6 TO 8 SERVINGS

Duck is traditional feast fare. Ready-cooked ducks are available at most Asian meat markets and are comparable in cost to a raw duck. Peking duck, one of China's celebrated dishes, usually requires ordering 24 hours in advance. This recipe gives simple instructions for basic roast duck. The meat then may be eaten as a course or used in flavoring fried rice or soup.

1   4 to 5 pound duck
    Hot cooked rice (optional)

Preheat oven to 350° F. Be sure the oil sacs above the tail are removed. If they aren't, cut a 1½-inch slit at the back of the tail and remove them.

Wipe duck inside and out with a damp paper towel. Place breast-side up on a rack over a drip pan containing several inches of water. Baste duck at 15 minute intervals. Roast until tender, allowing about 30 minutes per pound. Add more water to drip pan as it evaporates. Duck is done when the leg joints move easily.

Place duck in a colander and drain juices into a bowl. Let cool. Bone and cut the duck into 1×2-inch pieces with skin intact. Serve as desired.

Preparation time: 10 minutes
Cooking time: 1¾ to 2 hours

HUNAN CHICKEN WITH GARLIC

MAKES 2 TO 3 SERVINGS

1   whole chicken breast
1   egg, beaten
½   teaspoon salt
1   tablespoon plus 1 teaspoon
    soy sauce
1   teaspoon hoisin sauce
    Oil for deep frying
1   medium yellow onion,
    cut into medium-sized pieces
1   small green pepper, thinly sliced
6   cloves garlic, minced
¼   cup bamboo shoots,
    cut into matchsticks
¼   cup fresh mushrooms, quartered
3   dried black mushrooms,
    soaked 20 minutes in hot water,
    drained and sliced
1   tablespoon vinegar
1   tablespoon dry sherry
1   tablespoon sugar
½   cup unsalted roasted peanuts

Bone chicken, remove skin and cut into 1-inch pieces. Mix chicken with egg, salt, 1 teaspoon soy sauce, and hoisin sauce; drain excess liquid.

In a wok, deep fryer, or large skillet, heat 3 inches of oil to 325° F. Deep fry the chicken for 1 minute. Maintain 325° F temperature, then deep fry the remaining chicken. Drain on paper towels and set aside. Drain the oil from the skillet or deep fryer; strain out impurities and reserve for other uses.

In the oil remaining on the sides and bottom of the wok or skillet, stir-fry the onion, green pepper, and garlic for 1 minute. (If you used a deep fryer, heat 1 tablespoon vegetable oil in the wok or skillet and stir-fry as above.)

Return the chicken to the skillet and toss. Add 1 tablespoon soy and the remaining ingredients. Toss and heat through for 1 minutes. Serve at once.

Preparation time: 10 minutes
Cooking time: 10 minutes

KUNG PAO CHICKEN

MAKES 4 SERVINGS

A classic Szechwan dish of diced chicken and peanuts, seasoned with the fiery hot peppers of the region. While in China the chilies are eaten along with the dish, they are *very* hot and you may prefer to leave the chilies on the plate. Do serve them, however, because they are a colorful contrast to the chicken.

- ½ pound chicken breast, skinned and boned
- 1 egg white
- 2 tablespoons soy sauce
- 1 teaspoon minced fresh ginger
- ½ cup and 1 teaspoon peanut oil
- ½ cup green pepper, cut into 1-inch cubes
- ½ cup red bell pepper, cut into 1-inch cubes
- ½ cup bamboo shoots, cut into 1-inch cubes
- ½ cup peanut oil, for stir-frying
- ½ teaspoon sugar
- ½ teaspoon rice wine vinegar
- 1 tablespoon dry sherry
- ½ teaspoon cornstarch
- 1½ tablespoons soy sauce
- 4 whole, dried hot red peppers
- 1 teaspoon minced garlic
- ½ cup dry roasted peanuts

Cut the chicken into 1-inch cubes; set aside. In a medium bowl, combine the egg white, 1 teaspoon of soy sauce, ginger, and 1 teaspoon of peanut oil; mix well. Add the cubed chicken and marinate for 30 minutes. Meanwhile, chop and assemble the vegetables near the wok in the order they will be used.

In a small bowl, prepare the sauce. Combine the sugar, rice wine vinegar, sherry, cornstarch, and soy sauce. Mix well; set aside.

Heat ½ cup peanut oil in a wok or heavy skillet to 350° F. Stir in the hot red peppers and garlic; stir-fry for 1 minute. Add the marinated chicken mixture; stir-fry for 1 minute. Add the green pepper, red bell pepper, and bamboo shoots; stir-fry for 1 minute longer.

Stir the sauce if it has separated and then add it to the wok, stirring constantly until it thickens. Toss with peanuts and serve immediately.

Preparation time: 12 minutes
Marinating time: 30 minutes
Cooking time: 5 minutes

HAZELNUT CHICKEN

MAKES 6 SERVINGS

- 1½ pounds boned, skinned chicken breasts
- 4 tablespoons sherry
- 2½ tablespoons soy sauce
- 1 teaspoon sugar
- ½ cup cornstarch
- 1 large egg, well beaten
- ½ cup butter
- 1 cup coarsely chopped hazelnuts
- 1 teaspoon minced fresh ginger, or ¼ teaspoon ground ginger
- 1 clove garlic, minced, or ½ teaspoon garlic powder
- 1 8-ounce can sliced bamboo shoots, drained
  Hot cooked rice (optional)

Cut the chicken breasts into bite-sized pieces. In a bowl, combine sherry, soy sauce, and sugar; mix well. Pour marinade over chicken, cover and refrigerate a minimum of 1 hour, or overnight.

Drain the chicken, discarding the marinade. Dredge the chicken in cornstarch, dip in beaten egg, place on a cake rack covered with wax paper and let dry for 30 minutes.

Meanwhile, in a hot wok or skillet, stir-fry the hazelnuts in butter for 5 minutes; remove with a slotted spoon and set aside. Add the chicken to the skillet and cook with ginger and garlic until the chicken is golden brown on both sides. Add the reserved marinade, bamboo shoots and ½ cup hot water. Cover and simmer for 10 minutes. Add the hazelnuts and heat through. Serve immediately over a bed of rice, if desired.

Preparation time: 30 minutes
Marinating time: 1 hour or overnight
Cooking time: 15 to 20 minutes

GINGER CHICKEN AND MUSHROOMS STIR-FRY

MAKES 4 SERVINGS

3 tablespoons lemon juice
3 tablespoons soy sauce
1 tablespoon grated fresh ginger
2 cloves garlic, minced
2 skinned, boned chicken breast halves, cut into ½-inch strips
2 teaspoons cornstarch
⅓ cup chicken broth
  Vegetable oil
8 ounces fresh mushrooms, quartered
1½ cups asparagus spears, cut into 1½ pieces
3 green onions, sliced diagonally into 1-inch pieces
  Sesame seeds, toasted
  Lemon slices
  Hot cooked rice (optional)
  Chinese parsley (cilantro) or parsley sprigs

In a bowl, combine the lemon juice, soy sauce, ginger, and garlic. Add the chicken, tossing to coat. Cover and refrigerate for 1 to 2 hours, or overnight.

In a measuring cup, dissolve the cornstarch in broth; set aside.

Heat 1 to 2 tablespoons of oil in a wok or skillet until it sizzles. Drain chicken, discarding the marinade. Add the chicken and mushrooms to the skillet; stir-fry over high heat until the chicken loses its pink color. Add asparagus and onions; stir-fry over high heat until the chicken is thoroughly cooked and the vegetables are crisp-tender. Stir in cornstarch-broth mixture and continue cooking until sauce thickens.

Sprinkle chicken with toasted sesame seeds. Serve over hot cooked rice, if desired. Garnish with lemon slices and cilantro sprigs.

Preparation time: 5 minutes
Marinating time: 1 to 2 hours or overnight
Cooking time: 10 minutes

IMPERIAL CHICKEN WITH PEANUTS

MAKES 4 SERVINGS

2 large chicken breasts, boned, skinned, and split
1 tablespoon soy sauce
1 tablespoon dry sherry
4 green onions, cut into 1-inch pieces
1 teaspoon minced fresh ginger
½ cup orange juice
2½ teaspoons cornstarch
¼ cup peanut oil
½ cup fresh snow peas
1 red bell pepper, cut into thin strips
½ cup salted peanuts, chopped

Cut chicken into strips 1½ × ½-inch. In a medium bowl, combine the soy sauce, sherry, green onions, and ginger. Add the chicken and toss well; set aside. In a small bowl, combine the orange juice and cornstarch; set aside.

Heat the oil in a wok or large skillet. Drain the chicken and discard the marinade. Stir-fry the marinated chicken for about 2 minutes, or until the chicken loses its color. Add the pea pods, red bell pepper, and peanuts; stir-fry 2 minutes. Stir in the orange juice mixture and stir-fry until slightly thickened. Serve immediately.

Preparation time: 5 minutes
Cooking time: 7 to 10 minutes

SWEET AND SOUR CHICKEN WITH ASPARAGUS

MAKES 4 SERVINGS

- 3 tablespoons peanut oil
- 1 teaspoon minced fresh ginger
- 1 clove garlic, minced
- 1 pound chicken breast meat, cut into bite-sized pieces
- 1 cup chicken stock
- 3 tablespoons sugar
- ¼ cup cider vinegar
- 1 tablespoon dry white wine
- 1 cup thinly sliced carrots
- 1 pound asparagus, cut diagonally into ½-inch pieces
- ½ tablespoon cornstarch
- 2¼ teaspoons sherry
  Hot cooked rice (optional)

Heat oil in a wok or skillet and stir-fry the ginger and garlic for 10 seconds. Add the chicken and stir-fry until chicken turns white.

In a small bowl, blend chicken stock, sugar, vinegar, and wine. Add stock mixture to skillet along with carrots. Stir-fry for 1 minute, then add asparagus. Simmer about 3 minutes.

In a cup, blend the cornstarch with sherry until smooth. Add to the chicken, cooking and stirring until the sauce becomes thick and clear. Serve with steamed rice, if desired.

Preparation time: 10 minutes
Cooking time: 10 minutes

Above: Fresh poultry ready for the ride home via bicycle.

Left: Sweet and Sour Chicken with Asparagus.

SEAFOOD

海鮮

Common to the cooking styles of all regions is the important role played by fish–fresh-water or salt, finned or shelled, fresh or dried. The Chinese depend on fish and seafood as a source of protein. Since many kinds of fish and shellfish can be dried and preserved, it is easier for markets to carry quantities of dried ingredients than it is to carry perishable goods. Cooks then can use the dried fish even if fresh is out of season. One thing to consider when cooking with dried, salted fish is its strong flavor. It should be used sparingly, in sauces or as a condiment rather than as a main ingredient. The exception is dried shrimp and abalone, which may serve as accents as well as complete dishes.

The Chinese New Year falls on the first new moon after the sun enters Aquarius–sometime between January 21 and February 19. It is celebrated with fireworks and a fabulous parade. An authentic nine-course meal is often served, and generally includes seafood.

SHRIMP AND CASHEW STIR-FRY

MAKES 4 TO 6 SERVINGS

¼ cup cashews
1 pound medium shrimp, shelled, or strips of a firm fish such as monkfish
2 tablespoons soy sauce
¼ cup chicken broth
2 tablespoons dry sherry
2 teaspoons cornstarch
½ teaspoon sugar
3 tablespoons peanut or vegetable oil
1 medium yellow onion, cut into 1-inch pieces
1½ cups fresh snow peas, or 1 6-ounce package frozen pea pods, thawed
1 clove garlic, minced
½ teaspoon grated ginger
Hot cooked rice or rice noodles

Preheat the oven to 300° F. Warm the cashews for 5 minutes, turning once.

In a bowl, combine the shrimp with 1 tablespoon of the soy sauce, turning to coat; set aside. To make the sauce, combine the chicken broth, sherry, 1 tablespoon soy sauce, cornstarch, and sugar in a small bowl; set aside.

Heat 2 tablespoons of oil in a wok or large nonstick skillet over medium-high heat. Add the shrimp and stir-fry for 1 to 2 minutes, or until they turn bright pink. Transfer the shrimp to a warm platter.

Heat the remaining oil in the same skillet. Add the onion, pea pods, garlic, and ginger; stir-fry for 2 minutes. Pour the reserved sauce into the pan and add the shrimp; stir-fry for 30 seconds, or until sauce is slightly thickened. Top with cashews. Serve over rice or rice noodles.

Preparation time: 5 minutes
Cooking time: 7 to 10 minutes

STEAMED FISH

MAKES 6 SERVINGS

1 tablespoon peanut or
   vegetable oil
2 cloves garlic, chopped
½ tablespoon chopped fresh ginger
½ tomato, thinly sliced
1 yellow onion, thinly sliced
1 fresh green chili, seeded,
   deveined and thinly sliced
½ tablespoon fermented soya
   bean paste*
1½ pounds fish, such as sea bass,
   thoroughly cleaned
½ tablespoon chopped green onion
½ tablespoon Chinese parsley
   (cilantro) leaves, chopped

In a wok or nonstick skillet, heat the oil and stir-fry the garlic, ginger, tomato, onion, and chili for about 3 minutes. Add the fermented soya bean paste; mix thoroughly. Set sauce aside.

Place the fish on an oiled and warmed plate. Cover the fish with aluminum foil and pierce a few holes in the top.

Steam the fish for 8 minutes in a bamboo steamer. Carefully remove the foil and transfer the fish to a warm platter. Pour the fried mixture over the fish. Garnish with green onions and Chinese parsley.

Preparation time: 10 minutes
Cooking time: 8 minutes

*NOTE: Available in most Asian specialty markets.

SEAFOOD AND ASPARAGUS STIR-FRY

MAKES 6 SERVINGS

2 pounds salmon, orange roughy,
   shrimp, or scallops
2 tablespoons vegetable oil
10 ounces fresh asparagus, cut
   diagonally into ½-inch pieces
½ cup diced yellow onions
½ cup celery, cut diagonally
   into ½-inch pieces
1 cup thinly sliced
   fresh mushrooms
1 8-ounce can water chestnuts,
   sliced and drained
2 cups chicken broth
2 tablespoons cornstarch
2 tablespoons soy sauce
4 cups hot cooked rice (optional)
¼ cup slivered almonds, toasted,
   for garnish

Wash and clean the fish and shrimp. Cut into 1-inch cubes, if necessary.

Heat oil in a wok or large nonstick skillet. Stir-fry the seafood until the fish flakes or the seafood is done. Remove from pan; set aside.

Add asparagus, onions, celery, and mushrooms to the hot skillet; stir-fry about 3 minutes, or until vegetables are crisp-tender. Add water chestnuts and chicken broth. Heat, stirring frequently, until liquid starts to boil.

In a bowl, combine cornstarch and soy sauce. Add to vegetable mixture, stirring constantly. Continue cooking and stirring for about 3 minutes, or until the mixture thickens and starch is cooked.

Return the seafood to the skillet and continue cooking until heated through. Serve immediately over hot cooked rice. Garnish with toasted almonds.

Preparation time: 5 minutes
Cooking time: 10 to 15 minutes

DEEP-FRIED SQUID WITH VEGETABLES

MAKES 6 SERVINGS

2 pounds squid, cleaned and
  cut into rings
2 cups flour
  Salt and freshly ground black
  pepper to taste
2 cups peanut oil
1 tablespoon peanut oil
1 clove minced garlic
1 cup chopped bok choy
1 cup sliced bamboo shoots
½ cup chicken broth
2 tablespoons cornstarch

Dry the rings thoroughly with paper towels. In a shallow dish, mix flour, salt, and pepper. Dredge the rings in the flour mixture to coat. Heat 2 cups peanut oil to 350° F in a deep-fat fryer or wok. To test, a few drops of water should sizzle immediately on contact with the oil.

Using a wire skimmer, plunge the squid into the hot oil and immerse for about 3 to 4 minutes or until the coating turns a golden brown. Drain on paper towels.

In a clean, hot wok or skillet, pour 1 tablespoon peanut oil down the side. Stir-fry the garlic until it becomes fragrant, about 15 seconds. Add the bok choy and stir-fry for 1 minute. Add bamboo shoots and stir-fry for 1 minute. In a small bowl, combine the chicken broth and cornstarch, pour it into the wok; stirring until thickened. Add the fried squid and toss to coat. Serve immediately.

Preparation time: 20 minutes
Cooking time: 20 minutes

STIR-FRIED OYSTERS WITH SPICY SZECHWAN SAUCE

MAKES 4 TO 6 SERVINGS

1 pint shucked oysters,
  (extra small or standard)
1 tablespoon dry sherry or
  rice wine
1 tablespoon soy sauce
1 tablespoon tomato paste
1 teaspoon sugar
¼ teaspoon chili powder
1 tablespoon vegetable oil
1 tablespoon thinly sliced
  green onion
1 tablespoon grated fresh ginger
¼ teaspoon sesame oil
  Hot cooked rice or rice noodles
  (optional)

Drain the oysters in a colander and reserve liquid. Thoroughly pat dry with paper towels and set aside. Make the sauce in a small bowl by combining the rice wine, soy sauce, tomato paste, sugar, and chili powder; set aside.

Heat the vegetable oil in a wok or a large nonstick skillet over medium-high heat until it just smokes. Add the green onion and ginger and stir-fry briefly, about 15 seconds. Add the oysters and stir-fry for 45 seconds. Add the sauce and stir-fry for 3 to 4 minutes, or until the edges of the oysters begin to curl. Add the sesame oil and stir-fry 30 seconds longer. Serve immediately with hot rice or rice noodles, if desired.

Preparation time: 5 minutes
Cooking time: 7 to 10 minutes

BRAISED FISH WITH BLACK MUSHROOMS

MAKES 6 SERVINGS

12 dried black mushrooms
 1 clove garlic, minced
½ teaspoon grated ginger
1½ pounds firm fish such as halibut,
     sea bass, red snapper or rockfish,
     cut into 1½-inch pieces
12 whole water chestnuts
½ cup thinly sliced green onions
 2 tablespoons cornstarch

Soak mushrooms for 30 minutes in hot water. Drain and reserve liquid.

Heat 2 tablespoons of oil in a wok or nonstick skillet over medium-high heat. Add the garlic and ginger. Add the fish and gently stir-fry on all sides. Transfer the fish to a warm platter. Add the water chestnuts, mushrooms, and green onion. Stir-fry for 2 minutes. Return fish to work; add soaking liquid; cover, and simmer for 2 minutes.

In a small cup combine 2 tablespoons water and cornstarch. Add mixture to the wok and stir until thickened. Serve immediately.

Preparation time: 30 minutes
Cooking time: 10 minutes

FISH WITH BLACK BEAN SAUCE

MAKES 4 SERVINGS

 3 tablespoons peanut oil
 2 cloves garlic, minced
 1 pound carp or sea bass,
     cut into 2-inch pieces
 4 ounces firm tofu,
     cut into 1 × ½-inch pieces
 1 zucchini, cut into matchsticks
 1 carrot, cut into matchsticks
2½ cups chicken broth, warm
¼ cup cornstarch
 2 ounces black bean sauce*

Heat the oil in a wok or skillet. Stir-fry the garlic until it becomes fragrant, about 15 seconds. Add the fish and tofu; stir-fry for 3 to 4 minutes. Add zucchini and carrot, stir-fry for 2 minutes. Combine broth, cornstarch, and bean sauce. Add to wok and stir-fry until sauce thickens. Serve at once.

*NOTE: Available at most Asian markets.

Preparation time: 15 minutes
Cooking time: 10 minutes

Fishnets for sale in the Yunnan region

VEGETABLES

蔬菜

Chinese vegetable dishes are characterized by crispness, excellent flavor, and bright color. Depending on the vegetable and how it's cut, it may be stir-fried, braised, steamed, or deep-fried. The stir-frying or quick-cooking method has many advantages. First the wok is heated until hot. Then a small amount of peanut or vegetable oil is swirled into the wok, coating the sides. When the oil is hot, salt is added to keep the vegetables bright and then the vegetables themselves.

Stir-frying calls for the vegetable to be tossed quickly, then to finish cooking in the juices it generates itself, or in liquid which is added later such as water, broth, or sauce. The hot oil seals in the vegetable's juices, vitamins, and minerals.

Mastering the art of stir-frying requires patience and excellent timing, but the results are worth the effort.

CASHEW VEGETABLES

MAKES 4 TO 5 SERVINGS

- 2 ribs of bok choy
- 2 medium carrots, peeled, cut diagonally into 1/8-inch slices
- 1 small yellow onion, cut into 8 wedges
- 1/4 pound fresh snow peas
- 1/2 cup chicken stock
- 1 tablespoon cornstarch
- 1 tablespoon soy sauce
- 2 tablespoon peanut or vegetable oil
- 1 clove garlic
- 1/2 cup cashews

Trim the leaves from the bok choy and cut crosswise into 1/4-inch strips. Cut the bok choy ribs diagonally into 1/4-inch pieces. Trim the snow peas and remove the strings along the sides of each pod; cut large pods into halves. Set vegetables aside.

In a cup, combine the chicken stock, cornstarch, and soy sauce; set aside.

In a wok or large skillet, heat the oil with the garlic. When the oil is hot, remove the garlic and discard. Add the bok choy ribs, carrots, and onion to the skillet. Stir-fry over medium-high heat for 2 minutes. Add the onion and cook 2 more minutes. Stir in the shredded bok choy leaves and the snow peas; cook 1 to 2 minutes, or until the bok choy leaves wilt. Stir in the chicken stock mixture. Cook 1 more minute, or until the sauce is thickened. Place vegetables in a serving dish and garnish with cashews.

Preparation time: 10 minutes
Cooking time: 10 minutes

Mixed Vegetables with Hazelnuts

MIXED VEGETABLES WITH HAZELNUTS

MAKES 6 TO 8 SERVINGS

2 tablespoons peanut or vegetable oil

2 cloves garlic, minced

2 teaspoons grated fresh ginger

2 teaspoons coarsely chopped hazelnuts

1 small yellow onion, diced

2 stalks celery, cut diagonally

1 green pepper, cut into thin strips

½ pound green beans, cut diagonally into ½-inch pieces

½ pound mushrooms, quartered

2 carrots, cut diagonally into thin slices

1 small zucchini, thinly sliced

1 small bunch bok choy or chard

¼ pound tofu, cubed (optional)

Juice of ½ lemon

Soy sauce, to taste

Hot cooked rice (optional)

Heat the oil, garlic, ginger, and hazelnuts in a wok or large skillet. Add onion, celery, pepper, and green beans, and stir-fry over high heat about 4 minutes. Stir in the mushrooms, carrots, zucchini, bok choy, and tofu. Cover and steam until vegetables are tender, about 3 to 5 minutes. Add lemon juice and soy sauce to taste. Serve immediately over hot cooked rice.

Preparation time: 10 minutes
Cooking time: 8 to 10 minutes

ASPARAGUS BROWN RICE MEDLEY

MAKES 4 SERVINGS

2 cups brown rice, cooked
2 teaspoons vegetable oil or spray
1½ pounds asparagus, cut into
   1-inch lengths
½ yellow onion, diced
½ cup celery, sliced diagonally into
   ¼-inch pieces
¾ cup mushrooms,
   sliced ⅛-inch thick
2 tablespoons soy sauce

Cook the brown rice according to package directions. Heat the oil in a wok or large skillet over medium-high heat until the oil ripples. Add the asparagus, onions, celery, and mushrooms. Stir-fry for 2 minutes. Add the soy sauce and cooked brown rice; stir thoroughly. Cover and cook 2 more minutes, or until mixture is heated through. Serve immediately.

Preparation time: 45 minutes
Cooking time: 7 to 10 minutes

SCRAMBLE EXPRESS

MAKES 2 SERVINGS

2 cups chopped bok choy or fresh,
   cleaned spinach
2 tablespoons finely chopped
   yellow onion
1 tablespoon vegetable oil
4 eggs
1 teaspoon instant chicken bouillon
1 teaspoon sesame seeds
¼ teaspoon ground ginger

In a wok or a 1-quart nonstick skillet, cook the bok choy and onion in oil, covered, on high heat for 1 minute. In a small bowl, beat together the eggs, bouillon, sesame seeds, and ginger until well blended. Pour the egg mixture over the vegetables. Cover and cook just until eggs are set but still moist, about 2½ to 3½ minutes, stirring each minute.

Preparation time: 5 minutes
Cooking time: 5 minutes

BASIC STIR-FRIED VEGETABLES

MAKES 4 SERVINGS

1 pound assorted vegetables
¼ to ½ cup stock
1 tablespoon soy sauce
½ teaspoon sugar
2 tablespoons peanut or
   vegetable oil
½ teaspoon salt
2 teaspoons minced
   fresh ginger
   Hot cooked rice
   Almonds or walnuts,
   blanched, toasted, and
   coarsely chopped

Cut vegetables as desired, keeping uniform in size. Parboil starchy, or woody vegetables. In a bowl, combine stock, soy sauce, and sugar; reserve.

Heat oil in a wok or skillet. Add salt, then ginger; stir-fry until fragrant, about 15 seconds. Add vegetables, adjusting heat to prevent scorching. Stir-fry to coat the vegetables with oil and heat through.

Add reserved stock and soy mixture and heat quickly. Then simmer, covered, over medium heat until vegetables are done. Serve the vegetables over hot rice, if desired. Garnish with almonds or walnuts.

Preparation time: 10 minutes
Cooking time: 5 minutes

STIR-FRIED MIXED VEGETABLES

MAKES 4 TO 6 SERVINGS

2 tablespoons oil
4 to 5 cloves garlic
2 pounds assorted vegetables, such as broccoli, asparagus and green beans, cut diagonally into ½-inch slices
1 8-ounce can water chestnuts, drained and sliced
2 tablespoons soy sauce
Salt and freshly ground black pepper
¼ cup toasted nuts, such as cashews, almonds or peanuts (optional)

Heat oil in a wok or large skillet. Smash the garlic by whacking cloves with the back end of a knife handle. Remove peel. Add the garlic to the hot oil and stir-fry until fragrant, about 15 seconds. Remove and discard crushed cloves. Add the vegetables and stir-fry over high heat until crisp-tender. Add the water chestnuts and seasonings. Stir-fry another minute to heat through. Sprinkle with nuts and serve at once.

Preparation time: 10 minutes
Cooking time: 5 minutes

BEAN CURD WITH MIXED VEGETABLES

MAKES 4 TO 6 SERVINGS

1⅓ cups bean curd, sliced ½-inch thick
1 tablespoon soy sauce
¼ cup cornstarch
2 tablespoon peanut or vegetable oil
1 clove garlic, chopped
1 large yellow onion, sliced
½ head of cabbage, coarsely shredded
2 stalks celery, cut diagonally in thin strips
4 dried Chinese mushrooms, soaked and sliced
1½ cups broccoli, cut into florets
1 cup bean sprouts
1 cup stock
1 teaspoon sugar
1½ tablespoons cornstarch

Marinate the bean curd in soy sauce for 10 minutes. Coat the pieces with cornstarch. Heat 1 tablespoon of the oil in a wok or skillet and stir-fry the bean curd until it is slightly brown; set aside.

Heat the remaining 1 tablespoon of oil and stir-fry the garlic until it is light brown. Add all the vegetables; stir-fry until cooked through. Add stock, if necessary.

In a cup, mix cornstarch with 1½ tablespoons of water. Add cornstarch mixture, bean curd, soy sauce, and sugar; stir-fry until cooked and sauce is slightly thickened.

Preparation time: 10 minutes
Cooking time: 5 to 7 minutes

NOODLES

麺

Noodles are the primary staple of northern China and the secondary staple of the South. Chinese noodles are distinguished not only by their constituents but by the way they're prepared. In soups, sauces, soft-fried, or crisp-fried, noodles can be served in countless ways: as a side dish, a snack, a garnish or as a whole meal.

Since many recipes call for chilled, parboiled noodles, these can be prepared in advance and refrigerated until needed. Parboiled noodles will keep for several days when drained well, tossed in a small quantity of oil–about 1 tablespoon to keep them from sticking together–and stored in a tightly covered container or plastic bag.

Unlike American noodles, which are made from durum wheat flour and specified to contain egg, Asian noodles are made from hard or soft wheat flours and generally do not contain egg. They are sometimes made with starches or flour from other grain sources.

Asian noodles can be divided broadly into Japanese and Chinese types. Although a very small percentage of the ingredients, the use of salt accords the main difference between the two types. Chinese noodles use alkaline salts, of which a common example is Kan-Sui, a mixture of potassium carbonate and sodium carbonate. Chinese noodles typically use a strong, higher protein flour. When combined with the alkaline salts, the high protein flour makes a dough that is stronger and more elastic and a noodle that is chewier and more yellow than Japanese noodles.

Specifically, Asian noodles depend greatly on the plant origin of the flour ingredients, with wheat flour noodles being the most common. Other types use wheat flour in combination with mung bean flour or starch, potato starch or buckwheat flour. One unique type of noodle is produced completely from mung bean starch. Rice noodles are also available. Noodles are available fresh (raw), wet (boiled), dried, steamed, fried instant (ramen), and steamed and dried (alpha).

Noodles come in all shapes and sizes: thin, medium, or wide; square or round; long or short; in ribbons, rods or diced forms. Their color varies according to the ingredients used. Bean thread or starch noodles are optically clear; noodles containing salt are opaque and white; alkaline noodles are bright yellow; buckwheat noodles are brown. For premium white and yellow color, high grade flour milled from white wheat is used. Minor and optional ingredients, such as eggs or gluten, gums or modified starch, emulsifiers, preservatives, and dried spinach or other coloring agents, may affect color and texture. Preferences are associated with factors such as cost, convenience, taste, nutrition, tradition, and culture.

Starch noodles, made principally from mung bean starch and sometimes from potato starch, are popular in all Asian countries as vermicelli-sized strings. Consumption of starch noodles, however, is small compared to that of wheat noodles. Ramen, or "ramyon," noodles are now the most popular type of noodles in both Asia and the United States, where ramen or Asian noodle soups are often served as a main dish.

Asian noodles are low in calories, sodium, and fat (except fried noodles, which are 15 to 25 percent fat). Made primarily from wheat flour, they are high in complex carbohydrates, the preferred form of food energy, and are a source of soluble dietary fiber. Noodles provide protein, B-vitamins, and minerals such as calcium, magnesium, iron, zinc, and copper. A half cup serving of cooked noodles has about 60 calories, less than an apple or orange.

Most Asian food stores will carry the range of noodle types (perishable noodles will be either refrigerated or frozen), as well as other ethnic ingredients, such as Pyogo mushrooms. Fresh noodles will keep for two to three days at room temperature and up to 20 days if packaged aseptically. Wet noodles will keep for four to five days under refrigeration. Fried and dried noodles remain stable for four to six months; steamed and dried (alpha) noodles for up to one year.

At right: Chicken Chow Mein (recipe on page 55)

COLD NOODLES WITH CHICKEN, HAM, AND CUCUMBER

MAKES 4 SERVINGS

Yakko Mein, or Yecamein, refers to "an order of noodles" and is actually a one-dish meal. The noodles, served in large individual soup bowls, are topped generously with sliced meats and vegetables, and then a rich, tasty broth is poured over all.

4 to 6   chicken thighs, skinned
2   eggs
¼   teaspoon salt
1   tablespoon peanut or vegetable oil
4   cups chicken broth
1   tablespoon soy sauce
1   tablespoon vinegar
2   teaspoons sugar
2   teaspoons sesame oil
10½   ounces dried Udon noodles
1   teaspoon salt
1   tablespoon sesame oil
2   ounces ham, sliced in long, thin strips
1   cucumber, peeled and cut diagonally into thin strips

In a Dutch oven, bring 5 cups of water to a boil. Add the chicken; cook 15 to 20 minutes. Remove chicken and shred; set aside. Chill broth; skim fat from the surface.

Beat the eggs and ¼ teaspoon salt together. Fry the eggs in a hot wok or skillet greased with 1 tablespoon of cooking oil, turning and tipping the skillet to make a thin sheet. Remove the eggs and cut into thin strips; set aside.

Season the 4 cups of chilled chicken broth with soy sauce, vinegar, sugar, and 2 teaspoons of sesame oil.

To cook the dried noodles, bring 10 to 12 cups of water to a boil in a Dutch oven. Gradually add the noodles and cook uncovered, stirring occasionally for 12 to 15 minutes, until the white core of the noodles disappears. Rinse the noodles under cold running water. Place them in a bowl and toss with 1 teaspoon salt and 1 tablespoon sesame oil.

Divide noodles into 4 bowls and arrange ham, cucumber, shredded chicken, and egg over top. Serve the seasoned broth in separate dishes so the broth can be poured into the noodles just before eating.

Preparation time: 5 minutes
Cooking time: 45 to 50 minutes

COLD AND SPICY LO MEIN

MAKES 4 SERVINGS

Lo Mein means "tossed or mixed noodles" and calls for parboiled noodles (also previously drained dry and chilled) to be added, not to the hot oil and soft-fried as in Chow Mein, but directly to the meat and vegetable combinations, which have already been stir-fried.

8   ounces fine or medium egg noodles
1   tablespoon vegetable oil
8   ounces fresh asparagus, snow peas, green beans or broccoli, sliced diagonally
8   ounces fresh mushrooms, sliced
  Cold and Spicy Sauce (recipe follows)
3   tablespoons green onions, thinly sliced

In a Dutch oven, cook noodles in boiling water until done, about 6 to 8 minutes. Drain. Cover with cold water until ready to use.

Heat oil in a wok or skillet. Stir-fry asparagus until just tender. Add mushrooms; stir-fry 1 minute. Remove the vegetables from the skillet and chill.

In a large bowl, combine the noodles, vegetables, and sauce. Arrange on a platter and garnish with green onions.

Preparation time: 5 minutes
Cooking time: 10 minutes

COLD AND SPICY SAUCE

3 tablespoons vegetable oil
2 tablespoons peanut butter
2 tablespoons soy sauce
2 tablespoons water
1 teaspoon sugar
¼ to ½ teaspoon dried chili flakes

In an electric blender or food processor, combine all the ingredients and blend for 1 minute.

Preparation time: 3 minutes

CHICKEN CHOW MEIN

MAKES 4 SERVINGS

Chow Mein, or "fried noodles," is a casual Cantonese dish which calls for parboiled noodles (previously drained dry and chilled) to be cooked with other ingredients, somewhat in the manner of fried rice; that is, the noodles and other ingredients are fried separately, then combined and cooked briefly together just before serving.

1 pound Chinese egg noodles, uncooked
5 tablespoons cooking oil
1 teaspoon salt
1 pound broiler-fryer chicken breasts, boned and cut into ¼ × 1½-inch pieces
1 teaspoon sherry
2 cups fresh sliced mushrooms
1 cup bamboo shoots
1 cup Chinese cabbage, cut diagonally ¼-inch thick
1 cup sliced water chestnuts
1 medium onion, cut in wedges then halved
2 ribs celery, cut diagonally
1 green pepper, cut in wedges
1 cup fresh bean sprouts
4 tablespoons cornstarch
1 teaspoon ground ginger
4 tablespoons soy sauce
½ teaspoon monosodium glutamate (optional)
⅛ teaspoon pepper
1 teaspoon sesame oil
1 teaspoon oyster sauce
1 cup chicken broth, warmed

Place the noodles in a large saucepan containing 2 quarts of boiling, salted water. Cook 8 minutes; drain thoroughly.

Heat 2 tablespoons of the oil in a wok or large skillet to medium-high temperature. Spread half of the cooked noodles in the wok and cook without stirring until light brown, about 3 minutes. Turn the pancake-like noodles and cook the other side until light brown, about 3 minutes; remove to a warm platter. Add 1 tablespoon of the oil to wok and repeat with remainder of the noodles.

In the same wok, add the remaining 2 tablespoons of oil and sprinkle with salt. Add chicken and sherry; stir-fry about 3 minutes. Push the chicken to one side of the wok and add the mushrooms, bamboo shoots, Chinese cabbage, water chestnuts, onion, celery, and green pepper; stir-fry vegetables about 3 minutes. Add bean sprouts. Mix together chicken and vegetables.

In a small bowl, mix together cornstarch and ginger; stir in soy sauce to make a smooth, paste-like mixture. Sprinkle the chicken and vegetables with monosodium glutamate (if desired), pepper, sesame oil, and oyster sauce. Stir in the warm chicken broth and bring to a boil. Slowly add cornstarch mixture, stirring to make a smooth sauce, for about 1 minute. Serve Chow Mein over fried noodles.

Preparation time: 10 to 15 minutes
Cooking time: 25 to 30 minutes

SHRIMP-FLAVORED NOODLES

MAKES 1 SERVING

        3 ounces Ramen noodles
   5 to 7 small shrimp, cooked
        1 teaspoon finely chopped
           green onion
        1 tablespoon shredded carrot
        1 boiled egg, sliced in fourths

In a small saucepan, bring 2 cups of water to a boil; add the ramen. Cook uncovered for 3 minutes, stirring occasionally. Remove ramen from heat and stir in the soup packet seasoning. Serve with shrimp, green onion, carrot strips, and boiled egg.

Preparation time: 5 minutes
Cooking time: 5 minutes

MIXED VEGETABLES ON STARCH NOODLES

MAKES 4 SERVINGS

   10 medium dried Pyogo mushrooms
    2 teaspoons sugar
    4 teaspoons soy sauce
    7 ounces cooked beef,
       finely shredded
    2 tablespoons sugar
    2 tablespoons minced green onion
    2 teaspoons minced garlic
    1 tablespoon sesame oil
    4 teaspoons soy sauce
    7 ounces spinach stems,
       cut in 2-inch pieces
    1 medium carrot, cut into
       thin strips
    1 medium yellow onion,
       cut into thin strips
       Pinch of salt
    2 eggs, separated
       Pinch of cornstarch
   ¼ teaspoon salt
    1 tablespoon peanut or
       vegetable oil
    7 ounces dried starch noodles
    4 tablespoons peanut or
       vegetable oil
    4 teaspoons soy sauce
    1 tablespoon sugar
    1 tablespoon sesames seeds

Soak the Pyogo mushrooms in water for 20 minutes. Squeeze water from the mushrooms and remove the stems. Slice the top portions into thin strips. In a bowl, combine 2 teaspoons of sugar and 4 teaspoons of soy sauce. Add mushrooms and mix well. Set aside.

In a separate bowl, combine the beef with 2 tablespoons sugar, green onion, garlic, sesame oil, and 4 teaspoons soy sauce. Set aside.

In a saucepan, bring 4 cups of water to a boil. Blanch the spinach in the boiling water for 30 seconds, then remove the stems, rinse briefly under cold running water and drain.

In a lightly greased wok or skillet, stir-fry the carrot and onion until tender-crisp; season with salt. Set aside.

Beat the pinch of cornstarch into the egg whites and ⅛ teaspoon salt into both the whites and yolks. In a hot wok or nonstick skillet greased with ½ tablespoon oil, stir-fry the whites and yolks separately turning and tipping the pan to make thin sheets. Remove; cut into thin strips.

In a Dutch oven, bring 8 to 10 cups of water to a boil and gradually add the starch noodles. Cook for 5 minutes, until the white core of the noodles disappears. Rinse the noodles under cold running water, drain and cut them into 3- to 4-inch pieces.

Fry the seasoned beef and Pyogo mushrooms in a hot wok greased with 4 tablespoons oil. Add the cooked starch noodles and stir-fry for 30 seconds.

Combine all ingredients, except the egg strips. Place the mixture on plates and arrange egg strips over top.

Preparation time: 20 to 30 minutes
Cooking time: 15 to 20 minutes

ZHA-JIANG SAUCE ON COOKED NOODLES

MAKES 4 SERVINGS

NOODLES

2½   cups all-purpose flour
1   teaspoon salt
½   cup cool water, 68° F
1   egg
    Pinch of flour for dusting

SAUCE

¼   pound fresh boneless pork or
    ham, trimmed and cut into
    thin strips
1   tablespoon cornstarch
2   tablespoons peanut or vegetable
    oil
1½   medium carrots, cut into
    ¼-inch pieces
1   medium yellow onion, sliced into
    ¼-inch pieces
3   tablespoons peanut or
    vegetable oil
5   tablespoons brown bean paste*
2½   cups beef broth, warm
¼   cup cornstarch
1   tablespoon peanut or
    vegetable oil
1   medium cucumber, peeled and
    sliced in thin strips
2   boiled eggs, halved horizontally

*NOTE: Brown bean paste is
available at most Asian markets.

Sift together the flour and salt; beat the egg with 1 tablespoon of cool water. Knead the 2 mixtures together to make a stiff, smooth dough. Cover with a wet cheese cloth for 30 minutes to 1 hour. Roll and cut into thin strips. Separate by tossing with a dusting of flour. Commercial wet or dry Udon or dried Chinese noodles may be substituted for fresh, if desired.

In a Dutch oven, bring 10 to 12 cups of water to boil; gradually add the fresh noodles. Cook 12 to 15 minutes, stirring occasionally. Meanwhile, mix the pork with 1 tablespoon of the cornstarch. Stir-fry in a wok or skillet greased with 2 tablespoons of oil. Remove the pork from the wok. Add

3 tablespoons of oil to the wok and heat. When hot, add the carrots and onion to wok and stir-fry until tender-crisp. Add the pork and bean paste to the wok; mix evenly. Add beef broth to wok and heat.

Dissolve ¼ cup cornstarch in enough cold water (about ¼ to ½ cup) to make a thick mixture. Stir mixture into broth and boil just until broth thickens.

Drain noodles; stir-fry in 1 tablespoon oil for 30 seconds. Divide the noodles into 4 bowls and garnish with Zha-Jiang Sauce. Garnish with cucumber strips and boiled eggs.

Preparation time: 45 minutes
Cooking time: 20 minutes

Two girls enjoying noodle soup in the city of Kunming in the Yunnan province

RICE

飯

Rice is the staple grain of southern China. Rice in addition to being boiled or steamed, can be combined with various toppings, prepared as fried rice, or made into a soup called congee.

Fried rice, which originated in Yangzhou (Yangchow) province, is a versatile dish which combines cooked rice, green onions, soy sauce, sometimes eggs, and just about any other ingredient–leftover or fresh–that may be on hand. The ingredient that predominates gives the dish its name: chicken fried rice, roast pork fried rice, shrimp fried rice, etc. When many ingredients are included, the dish is called subgum–or "many varieties"–fried rice.

Since fried rice is essentially a dish of leftovers, many of its ingredients, being already cooked and moist, should be drained well before they are added to keep the rice from getting soggy. Fried rice is fairly dry and aromatic. Paired with a light and simple soup, fried rice makes a good lunch or light supper.

Rice soup, or congee, is a dish of equal versatility. Congee is prepared by simmering a small quantity of rice in a large quantity of water until a smooth, creamy broth is formed. Any type of rice is suitable: long grain, oval-grain, or glutinous. The softened rice may resemble a thin gruel or a slightly thick porridge. The Chinese call it "jook." Congee is eaten for breakfast, lunch, supper, and as a snack. It is always served hot, garnished with either minced green onion or parsley, and seasoned with soy sauce.

STEAMED RICE

MAKES 6 CUPS

2   cups while long-grain rice

*NOTE: This water may be saved and mixed with sugar for a thin congee.

Rinse rice several times in cold water until water is clear, not cloudy. Drain.

Place rice in a pan with 4 to 5 cups cold water. Bring to a boil, stirring occasionally. Boil for 5 minutes. Drain.*

Place rice in a bamboo steamer lined wtih cheesecloth. Pierce rice several times to create steam vents. Place steamer over boiling water and cover pan. Steam for 20 minutes. Fluff with a fork or chopstick just before serving.

Preparation time: 3 minutes
Cooking time: 30 to 35 minutes

BOILED RICE

MAKES 3 CUPS

1 cup white long-grain rice
2½ cups cold water

*NOTE: For fried rice recipes, refrigerate overnight before using.

Rinse rice several times in cold water until water is clear, not cloudy. Drain.

Place the washed rice and water in a 2- to 3-quart saucepan and bring to a boil over medium-high heat. Do not cover. As the water evaporates watch for small craters to appear in the rice. Cover with a tight-fitting lid and re-duce heat to simmer. Cook for 10 minutes; turn off heat and let rest covered for 15 minutes or more. Fluff with a fork or chopstick. Serve hot.*

Preparation time: 3 minutes
Cooking time: 30 minutes

SUBGUM FRIED RICE

MAKES 6 SERVINGS

4 slices bacon, diced
½ cup chopped yellow onion
1½ pounds chicken breasts, boned, skinned, and cut into ½-inch strips
1 teaspoon salt
1 teaspoon freshly ground black pepper
1 cup cooked green peas
1 4-ounce can sliced mushrooms, drained
¼ cup diced pimentos
3 cups cooked rice

In a wok or large skillet, stir-fry bacon and onions over medium- high heat until onions are transparent. Add chicken, salt, and pepper; stir-fry for 5 minutes. Stir in peas, mushrooms, pimentos, and rice. Toss lightly and heat thoroughly.

Preparation time: 15 minutes
Cooking time: 10 minutes

GINGER-CHICKEN FRIED RICE

MAKES 6 SERVINGS

2 teaspoons vegetable oil
2 teaspoons grated fresh ginger
1 clove garlic, minced
1 cup diced cooked chicken
1 cup snow peas, cut into 1-inch pieces
½ cup thinly sliced carrots
½ cup sliced green onions
3 cups cooked rice, chilled
2 tablespoons soy sauce
1 teaspoon sesame oil
⅛ teaspoon ground white pepper

Place a wok or large skillet over high heat until hot. Add oil, swirling to coat sides. Add ginger and garlic. Stir-fry until fragrant, for about 15 seconds. Add chicken, snow peas, carrots, and onions, stir 1 minute. Add rice; stir to separate grains with back of spoon. Mix well. Stir in soy sauce, sesame oil, and pepper. Cook until thoroughly heated.

Preparation time: 8 minutes
Cooking time: 8 to 10 minutes

GLOSSARY

ANISE, STAR (Bot Gok): Small, dry, brown seed cluster, or clove, shaped like an eight-pointed star. Licorice-like, it's used to flavor red-cooked meat and poultry dishes. The cloves can be tied loosely in cheesecloth for easy removal after cooking. Sold by weight. When ground, 3 or 4 cloves equal 1 teaspoon of powered anise.

BAMBOO SHOOTS (Jook Sun Yee or Jook Soon Yee): Ivory-colored, conical-shaped shoots of tropical bamboo, usually about 3 inches across and 4 inches long. Sold canned in Asian specialty stores. (Can sizes range from 4 ounces up.) Large wedges packed in water are best. After opening, drain and store in fresh water in a covered jar in the refrigerator, changing the water daily. Can be kept for about 10 days. In cooking, kohlrabi or celery hearts will approximate the texture but not the flavor.

BEAN CURD (Dow Foo or Dau Foo): Square, custardlike cakes of pressed, pureed soybeans that can be boiled, steamed, stir-fried, baked, marinated, pressed, deep-fried or eaten fresh. When eaten fresh with various dips or condiments, the Chinese call it "meat without bones." Its slight, subtle taste readily absorbs and complements stronger food flavors, so it combines well with just about any meat, fish, soup, egg, vegetable or poultry dish. Sold by the cake, usually ½ to ¾ inches thick and 3 inches square, in Asian specialty stores. Drain and store in fresh water in a covered jar in the refrigerator for up to 2 weeks, changing the water daily. Also sold by the pint and in cans.

BEAN CURD, DEEP-FRIED (Dow Foo Pok): Eaten stuffed as snacks or used in stir-fried and vegetarian dishes.

BEAN PASTE, RED (Dow Sha or Dow Cha): A sweetened purée of Chinese red soybeans used in steamed pastries and sweet dishes. Available in cans in Asian specialty shops, it will keep for months refrigerated in a covered jar, and may also be prepared at home.

BEAN PASTE, YELLOW: Salty, pungent ground soybean product, used to flavor used to flavor and preserve food. In North China, it's used as a dip for raw green onions. Sold in cans.

BEANS, BLACK FERMENTED (Dow See or Doe Shee): Small, black preserved soybeans, which are extremely strong, pungent, and salty. Used with garlic as a seasoning. Subdues the fishiness of fish and heightens the flavor of pork, lobster, beef, and chicken. Must be soaked. Sold in 3- to 4-ounce cans and 3- to 4-ounce plastic bags in Chinese specialty shops. After opening, store up to 6 months, refrigerated, in a tightly covered container or plastic bag. Add a few drops of peanut oil or flavorless vegetable oil or water if they seem to be drying out. In cooking, may substitute an additional quantity of soy sauce or salt.

BEAN SPROUTS (Gna Choy or Ngah Choy): Young sprouts of the mung bean, 1½ to 2 inches long. Sold fresh by weight and in 4- to 8-ounce cans. The fresh ones have parchmentlike husks that must be removed before using. Refrigerate fresh sprouts in water in a covered jar for up to 2 weeks. After opening canned sprouts, drain and store in fresh water in a covered jar in the refrigerator. They will keep for 2 to 3 days.

BEAN SPROUTS, SOY (Dow Gna or Dow Ngah): Tiny white shoots with pale green hoods, that are not actually the sprouts of beans but of tiny mung peas. Called nature's most convenient vegetable since they can be grown in a few days at any time of the year, they add texture and a delicate taste to meat, omelets, shellfish, salads, soups, and other vegetables. Spouts should be cooked only briefly, so that their crunchiness is retained. Because of this crunchiness, the Chinese call them "teeth vegetable." Available fresh by weight and in cans, which must be drained before being used.

BOK CHOY (See Cabbage, Chinese)

BROCCOLI, CHINESE (Gai Lan or Guy Lon): Similar in color to the familiar broccoli, but much more leafy and somewhat longer (about 12 to 14 inches), it has irregularly shaped stalks, large florets with yellow and white blossoms. Its taste is fresh and delicate. Can be stir-fried alone as a vegetable or with meat. Sold fresh by weight.

BROWN BEAN SAUCE (Min See Jeung or Mien See Jeung):

Thick, spicy, aromatic paste made from fermented yellow beans, flour, and salt. Adds salty, full-bodied flavor to foods. Used to season fish, beef, and duck, and also bean curd and bland vegetables. Since it always must be cooked, it cannot be used as a table condiment. Often used interchangeably with fermented black beans. Sold in cans of 1 pound or more or in jars in Chinese specialty stores. After opening, it keeps for months refrigerated in a covered jar. In cooking, may substitute additional salt.

CABBAGE, CHINESE (BOK CHOY, CHINESE CHARD, CHINESE GREENS OR SHANGHAI CABBAGE) (Bok Choy): A variety of Chinese cabbage that grows somewhat like celery but has 12- to 16-inch long smooth, white stalks and large, dark-green leaves. The Chinese call it "White Vegetable." Extremely versatile and popular, it has a clear, light taste, and requires little cooking. Can be stir-fried with any meat, poultry or seafood or quick-cooked in soups. Sold fresh by the bunch or weight in Asian specialty stores. Refrigerate in a plastic bag for about a week. In cooking, may substitute celery, cabbage or romaine lettuce.

CATSUP (Fon Ker Jeung): Surprising to Westerners, used often in Chinese cooking.

CHICKEN (Guy or Gai): A favorite fowl popular throughout China. It may be prepared in a variety of ways: stir-fried, steamed, simmered, red cooked, or roasted. Can be added to congee, soup, and fried rice.

CHILI PEPPERS (See Peppers, Chili)

CHILI SAUCE, CHINESE (Lar Dew Din): Hot sauce made with small, red chili peppers, apricots, lemon, and garlic. Used to season fish, pickled vegetables, and salted cabbage. Very hot; should be used sparingly. Sold in bottles.

CHIVES, CHINESE (Gow Choy): Members of the onion family with narrow, flat, green leaves about 6 inches long. Look like a cross between green onions and chives, and add a sharp pungent flavor to noodle dishes, eggs, and stir-fried beef. Sold fresh by the bunch.

CORNSTARCH (CORN FLOUR): A powdered corn product used to dredge fish and meat. Performs a number of functions, such as sealing in the juices during cooking, producing a golden-brown surface in deep-frying, acting as a binder with minced meat and giving coarse meats a smoother texture. When used as a thickener in soup, it must first be blended with cold water to a smooth paste. Sold packaged by weight.

CURRY (Gar Lay): A seasoning powder from India, introduced to China centuries ago, which is used in many seafood and meat dishes. particularly favored in winter. Often cooked in a dry pan over low heat before other ingredients are added. Must be stirred constantly to prevent burning. Sold packaged by weight.

DUCK (Opp): Fresh or frozen dressed Long Island ducks about 4½ to 5 pounds. Whole cooked ducks are available at Asian specialty markets. Strong flavored water fowl, suited to braising, steaming, and roasting. Adds flavor to soup, congee, and fried rice.

DUCK, ROAST (Shew Opp): Whole duck sold already roasted. It can be eaten cold, reheated in the oven or stir-fried with snow peas, other vegetables, lichees, and pineapple. Sold by weight, whole or in pieces.

EGGPLANT, CHINESE (Bok Ker or Bok Quar): White eggplant, similar in shape and texture to the more common purple variety, but smaller–about the size of a cucumber– less pulpy and more delicate. It can be steamed with fish or white bean cheese, braised or stir-fried. Sold fresh by weight.

EGGROLLS: Stuffed rolls that are deep-fried and eaten as appetizers.

EGGROLL SKINS (Chuen Guen Pay): Egg-dough wrappings which, when stuffed with minced meat and vegetables and deep-fried, make eggrolls. Sold in 5- by 8-inch sheets by weight. Sometimes available only in 5-pound packages. Can be rewrapped in smaller quantities and frozen for future use, but must be completely defrosted before use. Can also be made at home.

Man and beast on their way to work in Xishuangbanna

FISH, DRIED (Hom Yee or Hom Yew): Fish preserved by salting and drying. Some are immersed in oil; others are not. Includes many varieties, such as flounder, haddock, blowfish, and the sardine-like pilot fish and silverfish. Domestic dried flounder is relatively bland, the imported varieties are stronger and saltier. Can be steamed with ginger or minced pork, combined with red-cooked meats or cut in small pieces and deep-fried. Is often soaked first. Should be used sparingly.

FIVE SPICES (Ng Heung Fun or Heung New Fun): A coca-colored, ready-mixed combination of five ground spices (anise seed, fennel, clove, cinnamon, and Szechwan Pepper) sold by weight in Chinese specialty stores. Fragrant, slightly sweet, very pungent. Used in seasoning red-cooked and roasted meat or poultry. Must be used sparingly. Store at room temperature in tightly covered container. In cooking, may substitute allspice.

GARLIC: A member of the onion family, it is used in seasoning meat, seafood, poultry, and vegetables. Often used crushed or minced and cooked directly in hot oil to bring out its flavor. Should be purchased fresh by the bulb; the individual cloves should be pinkish and firm.

GINGER (Sang Geung or Sang Geong): Gnarled, potato-like brown root, about 3 inches long, which has a pungent, fresh, spicy taste. Used as a basic seasoning, it adds subtle flavor to soups, meats, vegetables, and sweet dishes. It is always used with seafood, as it neutralizes fishy odors. Sold by weight in Asian and Puerto Rican specialty shops. To use, lightly scrape skin and slice, then crush, shred or follow recipe directions. When a slice is specified, it should be about 1 inch in diameter, ⅛ inch or less in thickness. Whole ginger root will keep for a few weeks wrapped in paper toweling in the refrigerator. Peeled, sliced fresh ginger root may be placed in a jar of dry sherry and re-

frigerated for several months. Peeled, sliced ginger root in brine is available in cans.

GINSENG ROOT (Yun Sharm): Aromatic root plant with sweet, licorice-like taste, originating in Korea. Prized by the ancient Chinese aristocracy as the "root of life," its name derives from two Chinese characters meaning "human-shaped root." Tradition ascribes to it the power to cure everything from the loss of appetite to heart ailment; from barrenness in women to a decline in masculine virility. Modern laboratory tests have found it contains an ingredient effective in treating high blood pressure. When taken freshly from the field, washed, peeled, and dried in the sun, it's known as white ginseng. When steamed and dried, as it is for better preservation and for export, it takes on a reddish tint and is known as red ginseng. Used in one form as a soup ingredient, in another as a medicinal tonic, it is also exported in the form of spirits and tea. Very expensive.

HAM, SMITHFIELD (Gum Wah Tuey): Cured, smoked ham with a strong, distinctive flavor, sold already cooked. Not Chinese, but close in taste to Chinese ham. Available by weight or by the slice in Chinese specialty stores, gourmet shops, and some supermarkets. Will keep for several weeks tightly wrapped in foil or plastic in refrigerator. In cooking may substitute Italian prosciutto or Westphalian ham.

HOISIN SAUCE (HAISEN SAUCE, PEKING SAUCE, RED SEASONING SAUCE, RED VEGETABLE SAUCE, SWEET VEGETABLE PASTE OR SWEET VEGETABLE SAUCE) (Hoy Sin Jeung or Hoy Sein Jeung): Sweet, brownish-red sauce made from soybeans, flour, sugar, water, spices, garlic, and chili, for use in cooking shellfish, spareribs, and duck. Also used as a table condiment for shrimp, plain-cooked pork, and poultry. Sold in

1-pound cans and up and bottles. After opening, can be stored for several months in the refrigerator in tightly covered container.

LETTUCE, CHINESE (CELERY, NAPA OR TIENTSIN CABBAGE)

(Wong Nga Bok or Wong Lung Gna Bok): Crisp, tightly packed vegetable, about 10 to 12 inches long, that has firm, vertical, yellow-white leaves, tinged at the top with pale green. Can be eaten raw in salads Western-style, but is delicious stir-fried with beef or pork, or quick-cooked in soups. Has a distinctive but not strong taste, somewhere between lettuce and cabbage. Sold fresh by weight. Sometimes available in neighborhood fruit stores and supermarkets.

LICHEE NUTS (Ly Chee or Lay Chee):

Small, oval fruit with rough, red skin, white pulp, and large pit. Have a smoky, sweetish taste, and are eaten like nuts or candy. Sold fresh in July in Chinese specialty stores, or in 1-pound cans or dried in 10-ounce packets in Chinese stores and gourmet shops. After opening, refrigerate the canned variety in its own syrup in a tightly covered jar.

LONG BEANS (Dow Gok):

Light, green summer vegetable, resembling attenuated string beans. Used in stir-fried dishes, either diced or cut in 2-inch lengths. They lose their fresh taste and become mushy if overcooked. Sold fresh in bunches by weight.

MONOSODIUM GLUTAMATE:

White crystalline extract of grains and vegetables, said to enhance the natural flavor of certain foods, but has no significant flavor of its own. Considered a seasoning, not a chemical additive. Used in fairly large amounts by restaurants, food processors, and food service institutions. There are two schools of thought on its value for home cooking: one that it heightens flavor, the other that it's not necessary when food is of good quality and well-prepared. Can be added to any dish except sweet dishes and eggs. Must be used sparingly so as not to mask food flavors, as excessive use tends to give all dishes a mechanical sameness, a pseudo-taste. Sold in cans and jars under a variety of brand names. If a recipe is doubled or tripled, the monosodium glutamate should *not* be increased correspondingly.

MUSHROOMS, BLACK DRIED (WINTER MUSHROOMS) (Dong Koo or Doong Goo or Tung Kuo):

Brownish-black mushrooms from the Orient, with caps about ½ to 2 inches in diameter. Meaty, succulent, and savory, the large, thick ones with light skins, curled edges and highly cracked surfaces are best. Can be stir-fried, stuffed, braised, steamed or simmered. Must be soaked. Should be used sparingly, as 6 are the equivalent of a 6-ounce can of mushrooms. Sold by weight. A second variety is flower shaped, thicker, rarer, and more expensive, and is used in banquet dishes.

MUSHROOMS, BUTTON (Moo Goo):

Small, white, tender young mushrooms used in soups and delicate stir-fried dishes. Sometimes used fresh, but more commonly canned, particularly the canned variety from France.

MUSHROOMS, CLOUD EAR (BROWN FUNGUS, TREE FUNGUS OR WOOD EARS) (Wun Yee or Won Yee):

Small, crinkly, dried fungus, about 1 inch long and irregularly shaped. Must be soaked. Expands to 5 or 6 times its original size and becomes brown and gelatinous. Resembles a convoluted flower or well-shaped ear. Can be stir-fried, braised or steamed. Used in pork, chicken, noodle, egg, and vegetable dishes, often in combination with lily buds, it has a tender, delicate taste and a somewhat crunchy texture. Sold by weight in Chinese specialty shops. Store in a covered jar.

NOODLES, DRIED EGG (Gawn Don Mein):

Long, thin noodles no more than ⅛-inch wide made of flour, eggs, and water. Can be boiled, braised or fried. Combine with pork, beef, poultry, soup, and vegetables. Sold, by the pound, fresh or dried, in Chinese specialty stores. Fresh ones may be stored in plastic bags in the freezer for months or in the refrigerator for 1 week. In cooking, may substitute any other narrow egg noodle.

NOODLES, PEASTARCH (BEAN THREADS, CELLOPHANE NOODLES, POWERED SILK NOODLES, SHINING NOODLES, TRANSPARENT NOODLES, OR VERMICELLI) (Fun See or Fun Shee):

Hard, opaque, fine white noodles made from ground mung beans. Must be soaked, then cooked only briefly, as they absorb some of the liquid in which they're cooked and become translucent, gelatinous, and slippery. They have more texture than flavor, but readily absorb the flavor of other ingredients. Can be simmered in soups, stir-fried with beef, lobster, shrimp, pork, and vegetables. Should be served at once when cooked, or otherwise they become shapeless and mushy. Sold in long bundles, packaged by weight.

NOODLES, RICE FLOUR (LONG RICE) (May Fun or Mai Fun):

Noodles made from rice pounded into flour that look like long, white hairs. Are thin, brittle and opaque, about 5 inches long, and have a distinctive flavor. Combine well with fresh oysters, dried mussels, green onions, pork, cloud ears, and lily buds. Can be parboiled, steamed, simmered, and deep-fried. When deep-fried briefly, they become puffy and crisp, and are used as a garnish. Can also be stir-fried, but must be soaked first. Sold by weight in bundles.

NOODLES, RICE (STICKS) (Sha Ho Fun):

Thin, brittle, rice flour noodles about ¼-inch wide, dried in 8-inch looped skeins. Sold in 8- to 16-ounce packages in Chinese specialty stores. Will keep indefinitely.

NOODLES, WHEAT FLOUR (Mein Fun):

An alimentary paste, whiter and smoother than egg noodles, that is prepared in the same way but cooked longer. Usually boiled first until nearly done, then added to stir-fried dishes and soups. Sold packaged by weight.

OIL, PEANUT (Far Sung Yow):

Clear, golden liquid shortening made from peanuts that is a commonly used cooking medium for both deep- and stir-frying. Imparts a distinctive, subtle flavor to foods and keeps them from sticking. Can be heated to high temperatures without burning. Can also be used again and again without clarification. Sold in bottles and cans.

OIL, SESAME (Jee Ma Yo or Jee Ma Yow):

Strong, amber-colored, faintly nutty-flavored oil made from roasted sesame seeds. Generally used as a flavoring, it adds a subtle taste to soup, poultry, shrimp, turnips, stuffings, and cold dishes. A few drops will improve any dish, but should be used sparingly. Sold in bottles in Asian specialty stores. Expensive. It will keep indefinitely. Do not confuse it with the mild sesame-seed oil sometimes sold in supermarkets.

OKRA, CHINESE (PLEATED SQUASH)

(Sing Quar or Sing Gwa): Long, narrow, light-green summer vegetable the size of a cucumber, that is segmented lengthwise, with sharp, tough edges. It has a refreshing, slightly sweet taste and is used in stir-fried dishes and quick-cooked soups. Sold fresh by weight. To use, cut away hard, stringy edges, scrape the skin and cut in thin slices for stir-frying or triangular chunks for soup.

ONIONS:

Most frequently used is the green onion or scallion. The white root end is preferred, as the green top tends to be peppery, and is cooked directly in hot oil to extract its flavor. Both tops and root ends, minced or shredded, are popular as garnishes. Other onions used are: leeks, shallots, and Spanish onions.

OYSTER SAUCE (Ho Yo Jeung or Ho Yau Jeung):

A thick, brown sauce with a rich flavor, made from oysters cooked in soy sauce and brine, it has a fine bouquet. Used as a seasoning, it intensifies food flavors without imparting its own. Makes food smooth, rich, subtle, and velvety. Used with stir-fried meat, poultry, seafood, with congee, and fried rice. Also used as a table condiment with roast pork, fried eggs, cold chicken, and beef. Sold in 6- or 12-ounce bottles in Asian specialty shops. It will keep indefinitely.

PARSLEY, CHINESE (CORIANDER OR CILANTRO) (Een Sigh):

Medium-green herb with willowy stem and broad, flat, serrated leaves that is stronger and more distinctively flavored than the common frilly variety. Highly aromatic, its called "Fragrant Green" in Chinese. Used as a garnish for soups and cold dishes, as a herb bouquet for poultry and as a flavoring for chopped meats. Should be used sparingly. Sold fresh by the bunch in Chinese, Italian, and Latin American grocery stores and some vegetable stores. Store in plastic bag in refrigerator for a week. To use, wash, discard tough stems and chop leaves, or leave them whole. In cooking, may substitute flat-leaf Italian parsley for appearance but not flavor.

PEANUTS (Far Sang or Far Sung):

Raw, shelled peanuts (not salted or roasted), that are used in slow-cooked soups and also with chicken.

PEPPER, BLACK (Far Joo):

Ground black peppercorns used chiefly in seasoning noodle dishes and soups. Can also be heated with salt and used as a table condiment for deep-fried poultry.

PEPPER, CHINESE RED (Hwa Jo):

Aromatic red pepper flakes used in seasoning stir-fried dishes. Sold by weight.

PEPPER, SZECHWAN (FAGARA OR WILD PEPPER) (Hwa Jo):

Speckled brown peppercorns with a mildly hot flavor and a pleasant scent used with red cooked meat and poultry, Chinese pickles, and pepper-salt mixes. Sold whole, not ground, by weight in Chinese specialty shops. It will keep indefinitely in tightly covered containers.

PEPPERS, CHILI:

Green chili peppers used as a hot seasoning, primarily in Szechwanese cooking.

PLUM SAUCE (So Moy Jeung or Sheun Mooey Jeung): Reddish-brown condiment with sweet and pungent flavor made from plums, apricots, chili, vinegar, and sugar. Piquant and thick. Used as a table condiment with roast duck, roast pork, spareribs, and egg rolls. Also used occasionally in cooking. If taste if too tart, add a pinch of sugar. Sold in 1-pound cans and 4- to 12-ounce bottles in Chinese specialty stores and in gourmet shops. After opening, can be kept, refrigerated, for months. The canned variety should be transferred to a covered jar.

PORK, ROAST (Char or Ta Siew): Thick strips of barbecued pork prepared with spices and honey. Sold already roasted. Can be reheated in the oven, such as oyster sauce. Can also be cooked in soup or stir-fried with vegetables. Should be added at the end of cooking since it needs only brief reheating.

RICE, COOKED (Fan)
RICE, GLUTINOUS (STARCHY RICE, STICKY RICE OR SWEET RICE) (Naw May): A variety of short-grained rice which becomes sticky when cooked. Used with meatballs, as a stuffing for chicken and duck, and also in sweet congees, pastries, puddings, dumplings, and banquet dishes. Must be washed and sometimes soaked before being used. Sold by weight in Chinese specialty stores. Store in a covered container.
RICE, LONG GRAIN (PATNA RICE): Long, narrow-grained rice, most commonly used in south Chinese cooking. Absorbs more water than the oval-grained variety. Yields a larger quantity, a fluffier rice. Can be boiled, steamed or used in fried rice.
RICE, OVAL GRAIN (CALIFORNIA RICE OR SHORT GRAIN RICE): Rice with short, wide, oval grain that requires less water but a longer cooking time to produce the same consistency as long grain variety. Tends to be softer and starchier. Can be boiled, steamed or used in congee.

SEAWEED, DRIED (PURPLE LAVER) (Gee Choy): Dark purple marine plant that comes in tissue-thin sheets, 7 × 8 inches, folded in half. Called "paper vegetable" in Chinese, it must be soaked, then it doubles in size. Used in soup, it has a fresh, tangy, sea-sweet taste. Is highly nutritious. Sold in packages by weight.
SESAME PASTE (Jee Ma Jeung): Ground sesame seeds, similar in taste and texture to peanut butter, that is used in sauces and cold chicken dishes. Available in cans but also sold under the name of "taheeni" in grocery stores specializing in Middle Eastern products and sometimes in health food stores.
SESAME SEEDS (Jee Ma): Tiny, flat seeds, either black or white. Sold by weight in Asian specialty stores, in Middle Eastern and Italian stores, and gourmet food shops. Store in covered container.
SNOW PEAS (CHINESE PEAS, PEA PODS OR SUGAR PEAS) (Ho Lon Dow): Flat, pale-green peas eaten pods-and-all that add crispness and a subtle taste and color to meat, poultry, seafood, and vegetables. Very tender and require little cooking. Are always stir-fried to retain delicate color, flavor, and vitamin content. Sold fresh by weight in Asian specialty stores and also available frozen in 10-ounce boxes in supermarkets. Store fresh ones in plastic bag in refrigerator; use as soon as possible. To use, break off tips and remove strings.
SOY SAUCE (See Yu or Shee Yau or Sho Yu): Pungent, salty, brown liquid made from fermented soybeans, wheat, yeast, and salt. Enhances the flavor of meat, poultry, fish, and vegetables, and colors and flavors gravies, sauces, marinades, and dips. Comes in many grades and types, ranging in color from light to dark, in density from thin to thick. Specific types are: light, dark and heavy. Good quality soy is essential for good sauces and marinades. Many grades are available. The imported Chinese and Japanese sauces are best and are available in various-sized bottles in supermarkets, as well as Asian specialty stores. These are made slowly by a natural fermentation and aging process. Domestic soys, made quickly by a chemical process, tend to be highly concentrated, salty, and bitter. These must be used in reduced quantities. Chinese soy is available in the light, black, and heavy varieties. Japanese soy, made with malt, is somewhere between the light and the black.
SOY SAUCE, DARK (Chow Yau or Cho Yo) Dark soy sauce, made from soybean extracts, flour, salt, sugar, and caramel, is blacker, richer, and thicker than light soy sauce. It's used as a table condiment, and also in cooking when both full-bodied flavor *and* color are wanted. (See also Soy Sauce)
SOY SAUCE, HEAVY (See Yau or See Jeow) Heavy soy sauce, made with molasses, is thick and viscous. It's used more for color than taste, in the rich, dark-brown sauces of sweet-and-pungent spareribs and stir-fried beef and peppers. (See also Soy Sauce)
SOY SAUCE, LIGHT (Sang Chou) Light soy sauce, which is made with soybean extracts, flour, salt, and sugar, is light-colored and delicate. It's used as a table condiment and in dishes such as clear soups where soy flavor but not color is desired. (See also Soy Sauce)
SUGAR, ROCK (Bing Tong or Bung Tong): Amber-colored sugar used to sweeten certain teas and to glaze chicken. Sold by weight.

TANGERINE PEEL, DRIED (MANDARIN ORANGE PEEL OR ORANGE PEEL) (Gor Pay or Gwaw Pay): Dried, preserved, tan-colored tangerine skin that is used as a flavoring. Imparts fresh, subtle taste to meat, poultry (particularly duck), soups, and congees. Must be soaked. Should be used sparingly. The older the skin, the more prized and expensive. Some rare ones are said to be 100 years old. Sold by weight.
TARO (Woo Tow): Starchy, tuberous, rough-textured brown root about the size of a large potato. Can be stir-fried, braised with duck or steamed with Chinese sausages. Can also be shredded and deep-fried as a savory. Sold fresh by weight.
TURNIPS, CHINESE (Lo Bok or Lor Bok): Vegetable resembling large, white horseradish. Very subtle in taste. combines with beef, pork, bacon, fish, and shrimp. Can be stir-fried or braised, and also slow-cooked in soup and marinated for cold dishes. Plentiful and best in winter months. Sold fresh by weight. To use: peel and slice.

VINEGAR (Cho): Rice vinegar is used in flavoring soups and sauces and as a table condiment for seafood, meat, and noodles. It comes in three types: white, red, and black.
WHITE RICE VINEGAR (Bok Cho) is used with sweet-and-pungent dishes. **RED RICE VINEGAR** (Jit Cho) is used as a dip for boiled crab. **BLACK RICE VINEGAR** (Hak Mi Cho) is used with braised dishes and as a general table condiment. All are available in bottles.

WATER CHESTNUTS (Mar Tie or Mah Tie): Walnut-sized bulbs of an Asian marsh plants with tough, brown skins and crisp, white meat. They are called "Horse's Hooves" in Chinese because of their color, texture, and shape. Used as a vegetable, they must be washed and peeled. Can be stir-fried with pork, beef, poultry, seafood, or with other vegetables, and are also used in soups and cold dishes. Sold fresh by weight in Chinese specialty shops and in various-sized cans whole, sliced or diced, in supermarkets as well. Store fresh ones refrigerated for several days. After opening canned ones, drain and refrigerate in water in a covered jar for about a month, changing the water daily.
WINE: Used as a marinade and liquid seasoning, it flavors meat and neutralizes the strong taste of fish and duck. The Chinese use a yellow rice wine which doesn't travel well. A good quality, medium-dry or pale-dry sherry, *not* cooking or cream sherry, can be substituted.
WINTER MELON (Doong Quar or Doong Gwa): Round, green-skinned melons of varying sizes. The pulp is translucent and white. Its flavor most resembles zucchini or other soft-skinned squash. Needs little cooking. Can be stir-fried as a vegetable or combined with pork in soup. For banquets and special occasions, this soup is often cooked right inside the melon itself. Can also be glazed with sugar as a candy or sweet dish ingredient. Sold fresh in slices by weight in Chinese specialty stores. Keep in refrigerator for 3 to 5 days with cut surfaces covered with plastic wrap. In cooking, may substitute zucchini or cucumber. To use: remove rind with a sharp knife and discard, scrape out yellow seeds, then slice or dice meat.
WONTON SKINS (Won Ton Pay): Thin egg flour skins or wrappings, about 3½ inches square, which are stuffed with minced pork, seafood or vegetables. Can be deep-fried, pan-fried, steamed, or boiled. Boiled wontons are usually eaten in soup; the others are served with soy sauce and vinegar dips. Wonton skins can be purchased fresh by weight or made at home.

INDEX

PHOTO CREDITS

American Lamb Council 3, 34
Chilean Winter Fruit Association 23
Michigan Asparagus Advisory Board 43
National Broiler Council 53
National Live Stock and Meat Board 19, 27, 31
National Pork Producers Council 15, 38
Oregon Filbert Commission 49
Peanut Advisory Board 14
Rice Council 7
© Eric Skiba 1, 6, 10, 35, 39, 43, 47, 57, 61

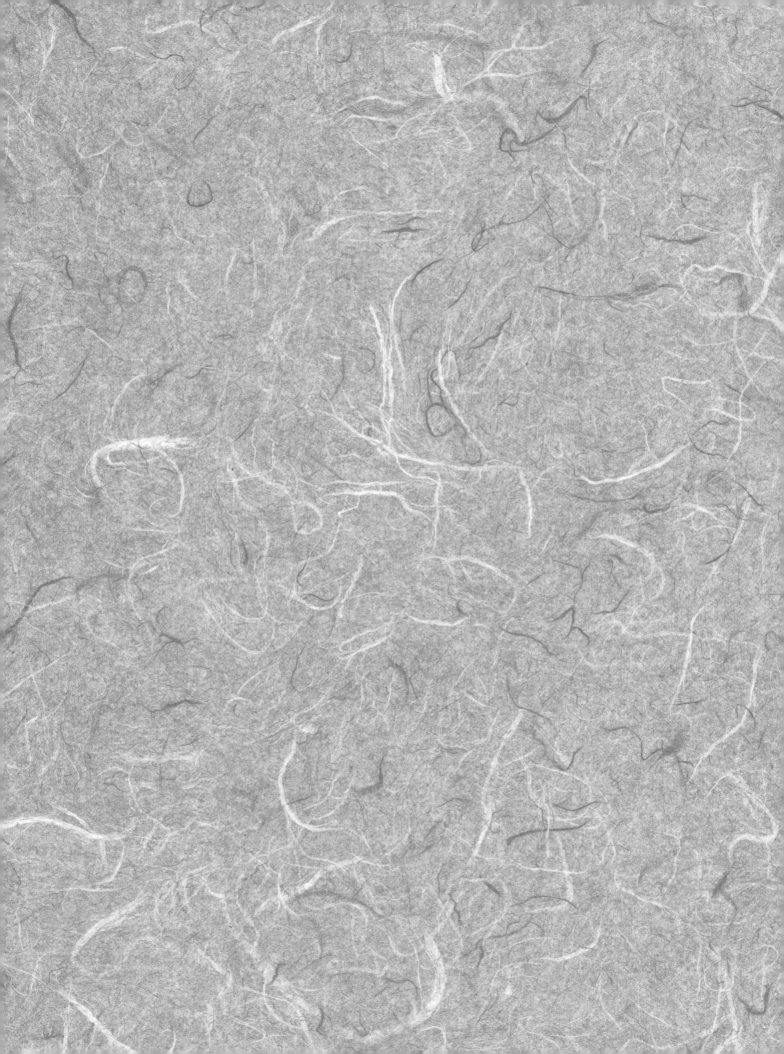